To Betty Hannigan: with much love Excelsior [signature]

THE POWER OF LOVE

40 YEARS OF
THE FUNCTIONAL LITERACY MINISTRY OF HAITI
(FLM HAITI)

by
Leon D. Pamphile, Ph.D
and Ervin Dyer, Ph.D

D1452920

FLM HAITI
EDUCATION · HEALTHCARE · HOPE

Love never fails

– 1 Corinthians 13:8

**...The amazing power of love
is beyond all comprehension
And it alone can heal this world
of its hatred and dissension.
- Helen Steiner Rice**

FLM HAITI
1064 Premier St
Pittsburgh, PA 15201
(412) 784-0342

FLM HAITI
EDUCATION · HEALTHCARE · HOPE

Table of Contents

FUNCTIONAL LITERACY MINISTRY OF HAITI 1983-2023

1983
- January 29: FLM faithful hold an initial meeting.
- Earns incorporation with the State of Pennsylvania.
- Earns 501(c)(3) status granted by IRS
- In December, creates Alliance d'Action Chrétienne (AAC), Alliance for Christian Action in Haiti

1984
- In January, opens the first five literacy centers with a budget of $500

1986
- FLM raises $11,000; opens 10 literacy centers with 344 participants
- Breaks ground for a community multipurpose center that becomes our guesthouse

1988
- Holds first annual banquet in November
- Opens the MIPADEP K-13 school

1998
- Meets the Rev. David Robinson, the pioneer of FLM's medical missions

2000
- In July, holds its first medical mission in Haiti

2009
- Celebrates the dedication of the House of David Medical Center

2010

- January 12: Earthquake strikes Haiti killing some 300,000 people
- FLM and Building Goodness Foundation (BGF) team goes to Haiti to evaluate earthquake damage
- September 14: FLM signs memorandum of understanding with BGF to build Boutilliers church, Thomassin volunteer residence, Thomassin replacement housing, and Thomassin trade school
- BGF secures funds to build the volunteer residence and the Boutilliers church.

2011

- In October: FLM's first cultural mission team travels to Haiti

2013

- In October: Excelsior Technical Institute is opened and dedicated

2014-2020

- Ongoing medical, education, and communications/cultural mission trips continue

2023

- October 28: Plans are underway for 40th FLM Anniversary Gala at the Doubletree Hotel in Monroeville, PA.

INTRODUCTION

One by one, the men and women of goodwill left their homes and braved the cold bite of winter to gather at the Lincoln Avenue Church of God. It was Saturday morning, January 29, 1983, when they gathered in the church fellowship hall in the Larimer section of Pittsburgh. There, they said their prayers and, in the name of the Lord, turned their focus to the socioeconomic problems facing a nation of people more than 1,500 miles away.

The group had come together to make an initial commitment to bring about positive change in Haiti. After discussion and prayer, the group, at the recommendation of Dr. Leon Pamphile, decided to address the serious issue of illiteracy plaguing the Haitian people.

Before long, the group morphed into a board of directors and gave birth to a new organization named Functional Literacy Ministry of Haiti (FLM Haiti). As they set to organize, the ministry was soon incorporated with the State of Pennsylvania and subsequently obtained 501(c)(3) status as an organization duly authorized by the Internal Revenue Service (IRS) to raise funds.

FLM Haiti is a faith-based organization. In general terms, a faith-based organization is one whose values are based on faith and/or beliefs, which has a mission based on social values of the particular faith, and which most often draws its activists from a particular faith group. Though FLM Haiti embraces the fundamental principles of this definition, we see our faith-based background as being grounded in the triple values of 1 Corinthian 13:13 – faith, hope, and love. These three graces form the triangle guiding and sustaining the organization.

FLM Haiti is grounded in the conviction that its growth and development is connected to faith in God. We rely solely on the words of Jesus that "All things are possible to him who believes" (Mark 9:23, NKJV).

This strategy has indeed worked as one considers the scope of service this ministry has provided to the disadvantaged in Haiti over these past 40 years. The first side of the triangle, confidence in God, is backed by the belief that God will provide the resources necessary for the operation of the ministry. We fully adhere to Paul's words to the Philippians: "My God will supply all your needs according to His riches in glory in Christ Jesus" (Philippians 4:19, NASB). FLM Haiti is a sure witness of the fulfillment of this divine promise.

The second side of the triangle points to hope. FLM Haiti ministers to a people where hope is often in short supply because of the oppression and ongoing violence prevailing in the country. Too often, Haiti is defined in negative superlatives, such as the poorest country of the Western hemisphere. Stepping in and working in this context of despair, we have to spotlight hope as a way out of this predicament. We believe that "hope fills [the heart] with eager expectation."

Anyone who has learned to hope will not be overwhelmed by discouragement. Instead, they will be filled with patience, encouragement, and perseverance. Hope is a key goal of the ministry as defined by its mission: "FLM Haiti aims to provide education, health care and hope to the Haitian people." We seek to open people's eyes to the prospect of a brighter tomorrow. We further reinforce this concept of hope through the programs we provide, backed with the motto: "Help Haitians help themselves."

The third and most important side of the triangle

is its foundation of love. For 40 years, FLM Haiti has been upholding love as the cornerstone of its ministry. As the apostle says, "These three remain: faith, hope and love but the greatest of these is love" (I Cor. 13:13, NIV). Throughout the years, FLM Haiti has consistently affirmed at each of its board meetings this motto of 1 Corinthians 13:8, namely "LOVE NEVER FAILS." We uphold the power of love as reaching out to serve others.

Now, love, as defined in the *Dictionary of Psychology*, is a "a complex emotion comprising strong affection, feelings of tenderness, pleasurable sensations in the presence of the love object, and devotion to the well-being of the loved one." Naturally, love permeates all of life's dimensions, such as erotic love, parental love, self-love that is self-esteem and self-acceptance, brotherly love. But here, we are focusing on the AGAPE dimension that points to "unconditional and unselfish love; the love of God or Christ for humankind, the love that shows concern for our fellow human beings."

In his sermon "The Three Dimensions of a Complete Life," Dr. Martin Luther King Jr. describes life as a triangle with three sides, comprising length, breadth, and height: "Now the length of life ... is the inward concern for one's own welfare. The breadth of life ... is the outward concern for the welfare of others. And the height of life is the upward reach for God." As King observed, "Somewhere along the way, we must learn that there is nothing greater than to do something for others." God's Word further teaches us that love does not seek its own good but the good of others (1 Corinthians 10:24).

FLM Haiti is committed to the "breadth of life" by motivating people of goodwill to engage in well-doing — to promote the welfare of those who are subjugated to oppression and violence. We believe like Martin Luther King that "a man has not begun to live until he can rise above the narrow confines of his own individual concerns to the broader concerns of all humanity." The Apostle Paul teaches us that love compels us to good work. "For Christ's love compels us, because we are convinced that one died for all, and therefore all died. And he died for all, that those who live should no longer live for themselves" (2 Corinthians 5:14-15a, NIV). We are bound to use love's powerful and Spirit-filled weapon to reach out to the poor and downtrodden of life.

FLM Haiti is a purpose-driven ministry, fueled by God's love, as bestowed on those committed to His service. It is staffed by change agents committed to pray, share, act, love, and to do God's work in serving the poor and needy, the disadvantaged. This book aims to share and celebrate the 40 years of service of the Functional Literacy Ministry of Haiti.

It will highlight the power of God's love to change lives through education, health care, and hope. It will also feature the stories of the valiant workers from the United States who, over the past 40 years, have committed themselves to relieve suffering in Haiti. They are our board members, our volunteers, our healthcare workers, and educators, who have devoted themselves as instruments of love and peace. They have all been sustained through the years by these basic tenets:

- Love always protects.
- Love always trusts.
- Love always hopes.
- Love always perseveres.
- Love never fails (1 Corinthians 13).

For a better appreciation of the loving service of FLM Haiti's ministry over the past 40 years, it seems relevant to establish the context in which the organization has been operating. We will thus begin by giving a brief introduction of the Republic of Haiti — with emphasis on its historical and recurring political instability, often resulting in dismal socio-economic conditions. We will then focus on the effort to launch the ministry and its steady growth as the result of its dedicated leaders and supporters here in the United States and in Haiti as well.

A note on methodology: This history of FLM Haiti is written from memories, organization documents, board minutes, letters, and oral histories collected from board members and other supporters. It is mostly written in first-person perspective, from the voice of Bishop Leon Pamphile, the founder of FLM. Therefore, any reference to "I," "myself," or "me" is a reference to Bishop Pamphile, unless otherwise noted.

FLM HAITI

EDUCATION · HEALTHCARE · HOPE

CHAPTER 1
HAITI:
A LAND CRYING FOR LOVE

At around 1 a.m. on July 7, 2021, Haitian authorities informed the world that a group of professional killers stormed President Jovenel Moïse's private residence in Pétion-Ville, a suburb of Haiti's capital, Port-au-Prince. The president was shot multiple times and had bullet wounds to his forehead and several to his torso. His left eye had been gouged out, and bones in his arm and in his ankle had been broken, according to one of the judges conducting the investigation. The president was shot 16 times. Haiti's first lady, Martine Moïse, was also shot in the attack and was evacuated to a hospital in Miami, Florida, for treatment.

President Moïse was assassinated by a band of foreign mercenaries, among them two Haitian Americans and 26 Colombian nationals, who authorities claim were recruited by a Florida-based Haitian pastor plotting to replace Moïse as president. The assailants apparently gained access to Moïse's residence by declaring that they were part of a U.S. Drug Enforcement Agency Operation.

In 21st-century Haiti, the barbaric assassination of President Moïse exposed the division and deep disunity that has beset the country throughout its history. Moïse's death came against a backdrop of political instability, with many key roles in the country's government already empty and the parliament effectively defunct.

Haiti's opposition parties have long called for Moïse to resign. Since he resisted, they turned to violence to end his presidency.

Geographically, Haiti covers 10,714 square miles (27, 750 kilometers). It is about the size of the state of Maryland. The island, which is the second largest in the Caribbean after Cuba, comprises two countries: the Spanish-speaking Dominican Republic and Haiti.

The original name of the island was Ayti, as given by the aborigines, the Taino (the indigenous people who inhabited the island before Spanish colonization). It means "mountainous country," as indeed, three quarters of the Haitian terrain is mountainous. The highest peak is called "Morne la Selle," soaring to a height of 2,680 meters (8,793 ft) above sea level.

Haiti is very prone to natural disasters. At the heart of this predicament stands a tectonic fault line that runs through the country, causing occasional (and sometimes devastating) earthquakes. In 2010, a horrible earthquake ravaged the capital city of Port-au-Prince and the Western area, causing approximately 300,000 deaths. In 2021, another earthquake hit southern Haiti, causing great destruction of property and loss of lives.

In addition, Haiti is also located in the Caribbean hurricane belt. In September 2008, four hurricanes and tropical storms – Fay, Gustav, Hannah, and Ike – slammed into the country with devastating force. Nearly 800 people were killed, 300 remain missing, and more than 500 were injured. More than 150,000 people were displaced. Cities and towns were inundated with mud.

Haiti has a warm, humid tropical climate. Temperatures are modified by elevation. Average temperatures range from the high 70s° F (about 25° C) in January and February to the mid-80s° F (about 30° C) in July and August. The village of Kenscoff, at some 4,700 feet (1,430 meters), has an average temperature of about 60° F (16° C), whereas

Port-au-Prince, at sea level, has an average of 79° F (26° C). In winter, frost can occur at high elevations. Haiti also stands out by the beauty of its landscape. When French colonizers settled in what became known as the Island of Hispaniola, they called it "La Perle des Antilles" (The pearl of the Antilles) because of its natural beauty. This factor, along with its warm climate, contributes to making it very attractive for tourism, which played an important role in the economy during the 1940s and 1950s. Unfortunately, much of the natural vegetation was destroyed through clearing for agriculture, grazing, and logging. Deforestation greatly accelerated during the 20th century as Haiti's population increased, and the forests that once covered the country have been reduced to a tiny proportion of the total land area.

THE COUNTRY AND ITS PEOPLE

Haiti currently has about 11 million inhabitants. Though there is the dense and populated capital of Port-au-Prince and other large cities, the majority of Haitians reside in the countryside. This population is predominantly Black, except for a small percentage of mulattoes who are the product of relationships between the former white masters and the African slaves. There is also a small number of Europeans, Asians, and Arabs who make their home in Haiti.

Haiti is known for being a rich cultural crossroads and bears the artistry (and other elements) of the different groups who have lived on its soil. First, the indigenous people, who were exterminated by the Spaniards, left many traces of their past. This is evident in the great number of words derived from their language that became part of Haitian Creole, which also borrows from African and French languages. The indigenous influence is also noticeable in some of the techniques that are still used in the arts of pottery and weaving. Finally, many religious beliefs of the Haitian people are directly inherited from the background and culture of the original inhabitants. As for the French, their contribution to Haitian culture is considerable. It shows up in social norms, manners, and artistic forms. However, the heritage of the language is particularly important. Since independence, the official language of Haiti has been French. However, in 1987, the Haitian constitution made Haitian Creole (Kreyol) an official language along with French. Kreyol is a French-based vernacular language that developed in the late 17th and early 18th centuries. It took root primarily on the sugarcane plantations of Saint-Domingue, which is what French colonists first called Haiti — and the language grew from contacts between French colonists and the enslaved Africans. Kreyol is the first language of about 95 percent of Haitians.

Above all stands the African heritage. Most Haitians are of African descent. The traditions transplanted from Africa to the islands by the formerly enslaved are easily perceivable in Haiti today. African culture is evident in the food, music, dance, religion, family life, and other areas of the daily living of the people.

HISTORY

On December 6, 1492, the explorer Christopher Columbus landed in Haiti, which he called Hispaniola, because the landscape seemed to him to resemble that of Spain. The Spaniards entered and landed in a beautiful bay that Columbus named Saint Nicholas. Columbus took possession of the island and launched one of the first steps to the colonization of the American Atlantic world and the disastrous inhuman sequel.

4

The first chapter of the European human rights nightmare in the New World was written in Haiti. As Spanish conquerors settled, fortune seekers came to exploit the newly-found gold mines and to cultivate the land. They enslaved the native people, forcing them to work in the mines and plantations. Following a century of forced labor and disease, the native peoples of Hispaniola were virtually wiped out. This disappearance created a serious labor shortage, not only in the gold mines but also on the burgeoning sugar plantations. The Spanish Crown identified the enslavement of Africans as the solution to this labor problem. In 1502, the first enslaved Africans were taken from a portion of Africa controlled by Portugal to Hispaniola. By 1540, the number had risen to 30,000 slaves.

Supported by their government, French pirates and buccaneers also came to make a fortune in Hispaniola. The slave trade, which subsequently emerged in 1503, was greatly intensified by the French, who later gained control over the Western part of the island after driving out the Spaniards. By 1789, more than half a million Africans were imported to Saint-Domingue (San Domingo) under French control. They endured the atrocity of slavery until a visionary leader named Toussaint L'Overture led them to a successful revolution against the colonial system. The bloody revolution lasted for more than a decade. With it, Black slaves and free mulattoes united under the leadership of Jean-Jacques Dessalines and defeated the expeditionary forces sent by French emperor Napoleon Bonaparte. And in the year 1804, Haiti became an independent country — the first Black republic of the world and the only colony to have won its independence through armed struggle.

The Haitian Revolution joined the previous American Revolution (1776) and the French Revolution (1789-1799) as a revolution that extended freedom and human rights. But there was a stark

5

difference. Though they proclaimed the ideals of freedom and the Rights of Man, both France and the United States remained colonial powers harboring slavery. The Haitian Revolution overcame the contradictions of the American and French Revolutions by extending freedom to all, regardless of race and ethnic backgrounds.

Haitians are rightfully proud of their country for being the first Black independent republic in the world. Haitians are equally as proud and gratified with the role their country has played in being a model in the struggle for liberation waged by others in the western hemisphere and in Africa.

DISUNITY

The Haitian Revolution is hailed as the most glorious period of Haitian history. One could compare this achievement to an ascent, namely "a climb or walk to the summit of a mountain or hill." In biblical history, there are "Songs of Ascent," a collection of 15 psalms that were traditionally sung by Hebrew pilgrims as they ascended the uphill road to Jerusalem, the ancient capital city of Judah. Reaching the summit, nestled in the Judean mountains between the Mediterranean and the Dead Sea, was certainly a symbol of satisfaction and victory. Once there, the pilgrims would attend before the Lord the three annual pilgrimage festivals of Unleavened Bread, the Festival of Weeks, and the Festival of Tabernacles (Deuteronomy 16:16).

Black slaves in Saint-Domingue likewise ascended to the mountaintop of freedom. They were able to remove from their island the awful institution of slavery. They achieved such heights when their leaders, Blacks and mulattoes, came together in a spirit of unity. It took place at a unique event in Haitian history known as the Congress of Arcahaie, where

Black and Mulatto leaders met: May 15-18, 1803. The Congress yielded the selection of Jean-Jacques Dessalines as the leader of the War of independence. It also gave birth to the Haitian flag, which became a symbol of consensus, national conference, and national agreement at the highest level to seal the future. For once in their history, Haitians made an incredible ascent that enabled them to defeat colonialism and slavery. They subsequently established the first Black republic of the world on January 1, 1804.

Unfortunately, this spirit of unity quickly melted in the heat of the Haitian tropical sun and political wrangling. During the 19th century, Haiti experienced a deep descent in political instability and socio-economic morass. Two years after the independence, its new leader and founding father, Jean-Jacques Dessalines, was assassinated on October 17, 1806. Civil war broke out over the process of his succession. The newborn country was divided into two States. The mulatto Alexandre Petion became president in the western and southern part, while the Black Henri Christoph ruled as king in the north. Chronic revolutions and civil wars beset the country through the 19th century. In 1915, President Woodrow Wilson used the assassination of President Vilbrun Guillaume Sam as a pretext to order American Marines to occupy the country. The United States stayed there as an occupying force until 1934.

After a few decades of relative stability during the 1940s and 1950s, Haiti fell prey to autocratic dictatorship. In 1957, François (Papa Doc) Duvalier ascended to the presidency following a violent electoral campaign. For 14 years, Papa Doc ruled with an iron fist. Haiti was marked by systemic human rights violations. Hundreds of political detainees were held in a network of prisons. Before he died, the dictator amended the constitution to make his son, Jean-Claude, his successor. Both father and son maintained power protected by a fierce militia, called the "Tonton

Macoutes." Both ruled ruthlessly, crushing all human rights values.

On February 7, 1986, overwhelmed by two-months of violent anti-government protests, Jean-Claude Duvalier resigned the presidency. When he boarded a U.S. Air Force plane bound for France, it ended 28 years of family rule. With his departure, Haiti returned to the instability that had marked the nation for many years before the U.S. Marine intervention in 1915. A new constitution was approved by a national referendum. And a presidential election, organized by Haitian Supreme Court Judge Ertha Pascale Trouillot, was held on December 16, 1990. It resulted in victory for Jean-Bertrand Aristide, a former priest of the Salesian order. His government was, however, short-lived. The Army deposed the new President after only eight months in office. On September 29, 1991, Lt. General Raoul Cédras commanded the bloody coup against Aristide, arresting him and forcing him into exile in Venezuela.

For some two years, the United States, the Organization of American States, and the United Nations led intense negotiations to restore Aristide to power. Despite various embargoes imposed on the country by these international organizations, the Cédras junta resisted any negotiated solution. On September 10, 1994, President Bill Clinton authorized the invasion of Haiti with a military force called "Operation Uphold Democracy." About 20,000 troops, soldiers of the 82nd Airborne, Marines on ships off Haiti, and commandos conducted the assault that dislodged the military junta.

Today, Haiti remains mired in political instability and violence. Poverty and inequality remain massive and deep, and economic disparity is wide. These problems worsened when, on January 12, 2010, a 7.0 magnitude earthquake struck Haiti. The devastation was incredible; it left the capital Port-au-Prince devastated. About 300,000 people were reportedly killed.

The government of Haiti estimated that 250,000 residences and 30,000 commercial buildings had collapsed or were severely damaged.

SOCIO-ECONOMIC CHALLENGES

Haiti's current challenge to provide for the welfare of its people remains tremendous. While Haiti was still recovering from the 2010 earthquake, it was struck by yet another earthquake in the summer of 2021, which devastated the southern peninsula. Haiti's economic and social development continues to be hindered by political instability, increasing violence, and unprecedented levels of insecurity. Economic recovery is also stalled by a highly polarized political climate. Haiti is facing a surge in killings, rapes, and kidnappings that are blamed on gangs emboldened since the July 2021 assassination of President Jovenel Moïse.

Haiti's socio-economic crisis was recently underscored by Martin Schüepp, an officer of the International Committee of the Red Cross, who argued there are too many people who are either directly affected by armed violence or who lack access to basic services, drinking water, health care, and education. Data from the World Bank indicates that Haiti remains the poorest country in the Latin American and Caribbean region (LAC) and among the poorest countries in the world. In 2021, Haiti had a GDP of $1,815 USD per capita (the lowest in the LAC region) and less than a fifth of the LAC average of $15,092 USD per capita. On the United Nations' Human Development Index, Haiti ranked 170 out of 189 countries in 2020.

EDUCATION

Education is officially compulsory for children

between the ages of 6 and 12. However, because of a lack of facilities and staff, a high level of Haitians lack an adequate education. Only 50 percent of children in Haiti attend school, making it more difficult to find employment in the future. In 2017, the Ministry of National Education and Vocational Training, together with the United Nations Children's Fund (UNICEF), found that more than 320,000 children aged 6 to 14 are not in school throughout the territory, and that about 160,000 adolescents aged 15 to 18 do not attend school. In total, according to the research results, nearly 500,000 children aged 5 to 18 are excluded from the school system in Haiti, and approximately one million are at risk of leaving the system without having finished.

Without a strong public school program, Haiti's school system is dominated by the non-public sector — whether for-profit, faith-based or run by non-governmental organizations. More than 80 percent of primary schools are non-public, enrolling more than 80 percent of all primary school children. Many of them attend private or church-administered institutions. Only about three-fifths of the adult population can read and write. The rate of illiteracy is higher in the countryside than in the cities.

HEALTH CARE

Haiti lacks a healthcare system that has adequate staffing, supplies, and infrastructure to meet the needs of the most remote and marginalized communities. In addition, there is a serious shortage of healthcare personnel, and hospitals are severely inadequate. There are only 25 physicians and 11 nurses per 100,000 population. Most rural areas have no access to health care, making residents susceptible to otherwise treatable diseases.

The National Library of Medicine reported that

only about 60 percent of Haitians have access to any form of healthcare services. Furthermore, according to the Pan American Health Organization (PAHO), most people rely on public facilities where they must pay a minimal fee based on income and family size. Most Haitians also lack clean drinking water, proper sewage systems and reliable electricity. Unsafe water — along with unsanitary living conditions — contributes to the high incidence of infectious diseases. The average life expectancy at birth is 50 years, and the infant mortality rate is 79 per 1,000 live births. The mortality rate among children under age 5 is 123 per 1,000 live births.

WELFARE

Haiti is typically identified as the poorest country in the Western hemisphere. Poor governance, corruption, and invasions add to an already unbearable burden for the Haitian people. Poverty in Haiti is manifested by the lack of services to the population. With respect to electricity, for instance, roughly 75 percent of households in the country are not connected to electrical grids. The few people with access to electricity in their homes face an extremely unreliable system, as the efficiency of the energy grid is approximately 50 percent.

In general, the dearth of social programs offered by the government forced most Haitians to rely mainly on their families and on the services provided by non-governmental organizations (NGOs). As has been true in so many other areas of life, Haitians have cultivated self-reliance in the face of hardship, scarcity, and the inadequacy of existing institutions. The Haitian diaspora is presently the backbone of survival in Haiti. The diaspora has actively participated in the developmental process of the country. Haitian remittances reached U.S. $3.1 billion in 2022.

Ultimately, the welfare of the Haitian people depends on the ability of their leaders to be guided by a policy anchored on the common good. Once again, we must go back to the effectiveness of unity that led to Haitian independence. Unity worked when leaders of the Congress of Arcahaie came to the realization that liberation from slavery hinged solely on a commitment to work and fight together. In 1807, the theme of unity resurfaced in the coat of arms of Haiti with the motto of *L'union fait la force* (Unity is strength). This motto contains the essence of the power of love because it implies that togetherness can bring about change. Through unity, Haitians defeated slavery. Likewise, it will take a united Haiti to conquer poverty and build a better Haiti.

Dr. Leon Pamphile, Rev. Sylvia Roaché, Bonita Ridley, Martha Domske, Dr. Bernadette Holmes, and Rev. John Bates

CHAPTER 2
LOVE ALWAYS ENLIGHTENS: EDUCATION

I was a teenager in Haiti when I witnessed an incident that forever changed my life. The angel of death had visited our neighborhood and taken with him an elderly woman whom I knew very well. Back then in Haiti, wakes took place after the passing of a person, and the rituals could be festive. The night before the funeral, people assembled at the home of the deceased. They played dominoes and cards, and drank ginger tea and clairin, a local alcoholic beverage. They also sang into an advanced hour of the night.

While attending the wake, I observed two men leading the singing. Each one held one side of a book, which they pretended to use as a songbook. Like everyone in the audience, I became enthralled by their enthusiastic singing. What I could not understand, however, was the fact that, for a good while, they kept singing different songs without ever turning a page of the book. I became so curious that I left my seat and made my way behind them to peek at the book they were holding. To my great surprise, these two gentlemen were singing from a car manual. It was their imperfect attempt to send to others the message that they could read.

From that day on, I was struck with the conviction to provide literacy skills to Haitians. This life mission was further reinforced by subsequent observations in my social environment. I was particularly aware of the weight of illiteracy in people's lives when I observed how it pushed them to lie about themselves. There was the case of a well-known and successful real estate agent who was quite impressive by his stylish demeanor. I observed him once when he was asked to put his signature on a document. He went instinctively through the pockets of his jacket, then of his pants, supposedly looking for his glasses. At the end of this rather painful search, he regretfully declined to sign because he said he could not find his glasses. What seemed to be an occasional bout of forgetfulness was, however, a scheme to cover his inability to read and write. For he knew well beforehand that there weren't any glasses whatsoever in his many pockets.

This mission of combating illiteracy in Haiti became even more compelling for me when I discovered in the Bible that Jesus was a reader. As He launched His ministry, according to the Gospel of Luke, "He went to Nazareth, where he had been brought up, and on the Sabbath day he went into the synagogue, as was his custom. He stood up to read," and the scroll of the prophet Isaiah was handed to him. Unrolling it, he found the place where it is written: 'The Spirit of the Lord is on me, because he has anointed me to proclaim good news to the poor'" (Luke 4:16-18a, NIV).

After a rather long trajectory of acquiring degrees in Haiti at the Law School, the Ecole Normale Supérieure (School of Education), and in the United States (at the Pittsburgh Theological Seminary and the University of Pittsburgh), I dedicated myself to living toward a vision of a better Haiti through education. I agree with Georges Jacques Danton, a French lawyer and a leading figure in the French Revolution: "After bread, education is the first need of a people."

Historically in Haiti, education has been compulsory since the 1860s. Yet in 21st-century Haiti, illiteracy remains a major problem. This is because

14

of a lack of economic resources and the absence of a national will to do more. Therefore, a large portion of the population fails to have access to any educational opportunities.

Dr. Pamphile awards certificates at a literacy graduation.

LAUNCHING THE MINISTRY

The initial meeting to focus on literacy in Haiti was held on January 29, 1983 at the Lincoln Avenue Church of God in Pittsburgh, Pennsylvania. Participants in this meeting were the Rev. Leonard and Sylvia Roaché, the Rev. John Bates, Sanford Chisolm, Martha Domske, Bonita Lee, and myself, Dr. Leon Pamphile, as convener. After a discussion of the socioeconomic issues in Haiti, the group decided to create an organization aimed at benefiting the people of Haiti. At my behest, they decided to focus on how to extend literacy skills to a people confronted with an 80 percent rate of illiteracy. The organization was named Functional Literacy Ministry of Haiti (FLM Haiti) to reflect this mission.

The group moved to build an organizational structure. We became a board of directors that engaged in drafting bylaws and rules of incorporation for non-profit organizations. We soon started exploring various means of fundraising. At the March 26,

1983 meeting, the board decided that its members would make a monthly financial contribution to the ministry.

**First two chairpersons of the FLM board:
Reverend Sylvia Roaché and Dr. Beryl Jackson**

Functional Literacy Ministry graduation service

FLM Haiti is fundamentally grounded in the Christian philosophy of caring for the spiritual and material welfare of the needy. As biological beings, we believe that men and women must be able to satisfy their basic needs. It is also our conviction that, as God's creatures, all human beings have the potential to achieve personal self-actualization. Furthermore, as heirs of the Judeo-Christian heritage, we also believe that to comprehend and apprehend the attributes of the Creator, the human mind should be enlightened — given the opportunity to know how to read and write. Throughout the years, we have been persuaded that the FLM vision is connected with God's vision to bring about good in the lives of the oppressed.

Alliance d'Action Chretienne board (AAC), who managed the work in Haiti: Duriel Clermont, Pastor Devese Pamphile, Pastor Roosevelt, Jean-Baptiste, Pastor Luc Deratus, and Pastor Bossier Jerome

PROMOTING LITERACY

As well expressed by the name of the organization, the board set out in the early years to focus on developing a literacy program to benefit Haitians. The primary objective of this program was to enable individuals to acquire and use the skills of reading, writing, and math in everyday situations. The board deeply felt that being literate enabled individuals to find jobs, enhance their living conditions, and contribute to economic development. They believed that literacy could even save Haitian lives in many situations (such as the ability to read signs or a doctor's order on a medication bottle, and to handle their everyday business).

The board also saw illiteracy as a stumbling block to personal development. Illiteracy prevents people from taking full possession of God's promises for their lives. Illiteracy exposes people to abuses of all kinds. Illiteracy further impedes national progress and economic development. When we started the project, this was the unfortunate reality for 80 percent of Haitians. FLM came into being because its leaders came to the full realization that it is far better to light a candle than to curse the darkness.

Having laid in Pittsburgh the philosophical and organizational structure of the ministry, it was then time to take the message to Haiti. It happened on December 21, 1983 when I traveled to Port-au-Prince for an initial meeting with Haitian leaders. The attendees agreed to form a board in Haiti and establish the first set of literacy centers. The new organization was named Alliance d'Action Chrétienne (Alliance for Christian Action), or AAC, with the motto "Christ, love and service." The new board of directors, made up of nine people, was established with Bishop Lopez Dautruche of the Church of God in Christ as president. He was assisted by Pastor Joseph Simon of the Nazarene Church as vice president. The power of faith permeated the groundwork of this meeting. It was highlighted that "believing is seeing," and the horizon looked bright if the word "impossible" was removed from our vocabulary. We began to think in a positive manner.

Our newly established board opened four literacy centers. Three of them were set up in Port-au-Prince, the capital city, and the other one was in Thomassin, which would become the center of our operation in Haiti. Located in the mountains above Port-au-Prince, Thomassin was then a close-knit community of farmers who made a living by tilling the land.

Education was offered only at a two-room elementary schoolhouse, which I attended for six years. After I left for better schooling in Port-au-Prince, I became a trailblazer as the first one from my village to ever complete a secondary education.

After decades of absence, I returned very enthused to promote education in the area. The response was tremendous as we opened one of the first literacy centers at my father's church. It had an enrollment of 55 men and women.

The first fruit from that center was, for me, very personal. The very first class included my mother. She was 65 when she acquired reading and writing skills. I remember being elated when she first told me that she could read the Bible well enough to help my father prepare his sermon.

FLM reached out to all in various communities. The age range in our literacy centers was 12 to 69, and the students were from the Catholic and Protestant faiths. The literacy effort was launched as a pilot project for a period of seven months, at which time we would make evaluation and adjustments. By the end of 1984, the Functional Literacy Ministry was well established in Pittsburgh and gaining an increasing number of supporters. The same was also true in Haiti with the setting up of FLM's AAC board and the operation of seven literacy centers.

PASTOR JOSEPH SIMON

The birth and growth of FLM Haiti rested for a great part on the shoulders of some key leaders, both in America and Haiti, who wholeheartedly dedicated themselves to the organization.

It has been said that "a little spark kindles a great fire." This thought can surely be applied to the contribution of Pastor Joseph Simon, who helped launch FLM Haiti. Simon first joined the newly established

Nazarene denomination in Haiti. After a few years, he founded his own house of worship, the Free Nazarene Church, which grew and soon expanded to other provinces in the country.

Pastor Joseph Simon, who helped to launch the ministry both in Haiti and in the United States.

His commitment was hugely effective both in Haiti and in Pittsburgh. As vice president of the Alliance d'Action Chrétienne, Simon served as a vital link between the Pittsburgh and Haitian boards. He kept us abreast of current events in Haiti, especially regarding political instability following the downfall of the Duvalier dynasty in 1986.

Simon came to Pittsburgh for the first time in March 1984. His visit was a stimulating boost to the emerging FLM work. Using the text, "My people are destroyed for lack of knowledge" (Hosea 4:6, NKJV), he made a forceful argument for the promotion of literacy in Haiti. Through his messages, hundreds of people became acquainted with our mission. Thousands more were reached through our first presentation on

Cornerstone TV. Pastor Simon inspired many to become monthly contributors, a strategy that remains the cornerstone of fundraising for the ministry. FLM Haiti has made it through the years by relying on individual contributions, with some donors having commitments dating back to 1983.

A year later (in April 1985), Simon returned to Pittsburgh and he spoke at seven churches in the area. At a service at the Church of our Savior on the North Side, we met a young man who was illiterate and unemployed. He was so touched by the FLM vision for literacy that after the service he ran home and brought back $20 to support the work. He then pledged to give $2 a month. The literacy program continued to advance through the years with the dynamic efforts of Pastor Simon. He organized regular seminars for teachers and visited the literacy centers.

On May 1, 1984, in the midst of an ongoing political crisis in Haiti, Pastor Simon wrote: "We are going through difficult times in Haiti, but that has not prevented us from continuing to work. The centers are functioning, and we meet every month with the teachers to motivate them to keep their responsibility."

In 1985, in another visit to Pittsburgh, Pastor Simon met with the board to share the development of the literacy program. He reported that the teaching took place in the Haitian Creole language and used such materials as a Bible, hymnals and storybooks. This portion of the program took two years to complete. The third step would include the teaching of reading in French. According to an evaluation conducted by Pastor Simon in May 1985, some comments emerged from the literacy learners that were quite inspiring. To the question, "Why do you want to learn how to read and write?", some of the answers were quite meaningful:

- I want to acquire more knowledge.
- I want to be able to explain everything.

- I want to understand the written word.
- I want to be able to read the Bible.

These answers represent the basic human longing for knowledge, for self-improvement and self-fulfillment. It became so relevant for us that FLM had to continue to do its best to respond to the needs of our brothers and sisters in Haiti. The result was also concrete. During a later trip to Haiti, I was uplifted by the testimony of Michel Joseph, a mason contractor who told me, "I am able to do my own payroll and write my own letters." As a matter of fact, there was a wave of enthusiasm for the literacy program. In 1986, the supervisor of our literacy centers, Henri Jean-Baptiste, composed a song to promote literacy, stating:

Long live literacy.

We know how to read and write.

Literacy is the only way to development;

Go to your nearest literacy center —

Learn about your country's history,

And Haiti will be on the move.

After three years of hard work involving both our American and Haitian boards, it was time to hold our first graduation. It took place on June 29, 1986, in Port-au-Prince, at the Central Church of God in Christ. What a great joy it was to be in the company of some 400 people: students, parents, and supporters of the program. The graduation was filled with a spirit of enthusiasm and reflected all the signs of a great festivity. Musical groups lifted the atmosphere with praise to the Lord.

There were 125 students promoted from level 1 to level 2; then 51 students who completed the second cycle expressed the desire to continue their studies. Plans were made to assist them in making the transition from Creole to French. There were 50 French transition primers purchased for that purpose. Above all, we gave each graduate a certificate of achievement accompanied by a Bible and a "chant d'Esperance" (songs of hope), which they could use at church and for their personal devotion. This was indeed what our program was all about — a commitment to bring a sense of hope to every life we happened to touch.

From then on, graduation became an annual routine. On Sunday, August 13, 1989, it took place at Pastor Simon's church in Port-au-Prince. The affair was a celebration with music provided by two church choirs. There were 111 students from the first and second cycles who were awarded certificates. Representatives from various centers expressed their deepest gratitude for the opportunity to acquire new skills that would enable them to pursue a new way of life. The literacy program continued to grow by leaps and bounds. Some 19 years later, for the academic year 2007-2008, we had 40 literacy centers with 1,200 participants. In the following year, 2008-2009, the literacy program consisted of 45 centers with 1,357 participants. The program reached its heights in 2009, when we had 60 centers with 2,000 participants.

SPONSORSHIP OF STUDENTS

Along with literacy primarily geared to adults, FLM gave special attention to children and young people by supporting students with monthly scholarships to attend private schools in the community. This initiative became a reality after I received many requests from parents to get sponsors to help with tuition for their children. I came to realize a vital need to add a new dimension to our ministry. When I shared the need in Pittsburgh, the response was positive.

Many volunteered to sponsor students in Haiti. We then identified many kids to help with their education. FLM paid their tuition to attend schools, and helped their parents in supporting their daily needs. This program was maintained for years, and many young people benefited from it.

MULTIPURPOSE CENTER

While visiting our literacy center in Laboule, a community adjacent to Thomassin, I attended a class with about 60 dedicated students. As a result, I got the vision to build a community center to increase the students' opportunities for learning. I soon shared this idea with Sheila Archie, a teacher and a member of Clark Memorial Church in Homestead, a community close to Pittsburgh. Sheila became interested in FLM through her desire to promote education. She became an ardent supporter of the ministry, was very involved with the literacy program, and thought that building a multipurpose center could provide a permanent home for the program! Classes were then being held in a house that was much too small. This building would not only serve as a literacy center, but also as an appropriate place for a Home Economics program (which was designed to teach skills that could help participants make a living, such as sewing, embroidery, artifacts, etc.).

Over the summer of 1986, we initiated the process to build this multipurpose community center. My father, Pastor Devese Pamphile, gave the land for such a project. I contacted an architect who drew up the plans and the securing of the funds for this project was committed to the Lord. The board stood then on Hebrews 11:33-34 (KJV), "Who through faith subdued kingdoms, wrought righteousness, obtained promises, stopped the mouths of lions. Quenched the violence of fire, escaped the edge of the sword, out of weakness were made strong, waxed valiant in fight, turned to flight the armies of the aliens." The board pledged to continue its effort in prayer, action, sacrifice, and hope.

Our prayers were answered through the generosity of Barbara Kunschner, a resident of Murrysville, a community not far from Pittsburgh. She became acquainted with the work of the Functional Literacy Ministry when she watched our presentation on Cornerstone TV. She wrote to me to express her desire to support our program. She soon became involved in our ministry and served on the board for many years. Kunschner endorsed the idea of a multipurpose center to help women in the Thomassin community acquire marketable skills. She generously supported the project from the beginning. Over time, the center became the hub and central location of FLM's on-the-ground operation.

On August 15, 1989, the dedication of the multipurpose center took place. It was the fulfillment of a long-anticipated idea, which at first seemed impossible. Deep gratitude was expressed to those who provided the finances. It was, above all, an opportunity to express thanksgiving to the Lord for His faithfulness. For all her efforts and generosity, the center became the Kunschner Center in recognition of the generous help she provided.

The center began by offering sewing, embroidering, and other marketable skills for girls and women in the community. By October, 1990, there were 40 students in the sewing and cooking programs. In 1992, these students passed successfully the exam administered by the Haitian government, and our program was then fully recognized by the government. When I visited in 1995, students made an impressive collection of crocheted items, such as lace, tablecloths and ornaments for tables, and we tried to find an outlet where these products could be sold.

MIPADEP

In May 1991, I came back from Haiti with a request to make the maximum use of the Kunschner Center by opening an elementary school there. It would operate in the morning, and the vocational programs would function in the afternoon. At the board meeting of June 8, 1991, it was decided that FLM would move in that direction. The school opened its doors in October 1991 with an enrollment of 50 students. Though this addition increased the monthly grant we would need to make to Haiti, we resolved to move by faith, being persuaded that the Lord would provide the necessary funds.

We call the school "MIPADEP" — an acronym for L'ecole Mixte Devese Pamphile. It is named for my father, who donated the land on which the school sits. Since it opened, attendance at the elementary school has exponentially increased. In the fall of 1992, enrollment grew to 175 students, which meant we needed to increment the teaching staff. It also became necessary to expand the building. In 1993, we undertook a second phase of construction in Haiti to add five new classrooms. This was possible, in part, because of the careful management of the Haitian board, which was able to save $4,000 as a down payment on the project. The expectation was to complete the project by the summer of 1993, as part of the 10th anniversary celebration of FLM.

Students from the MIPADEP school, established by FLM Haiti

Enrollment continued to increase at the school. In October 1999, the new academic year got underway at both the literacy centers and the multipurpose Kunschner Center. The school expanded with a secondary-grade section of 35 students. This addition was self-supporting since students would pay tuition. The Rev. David Robinson, of Crossroads Presbyterian Church in Washington, Pennsylvania, came up with the idea of feeding the students at MIPADEP. He approached the Washington Presbytery to secure funds for this purpose. Finleyville Presbyterian Church and the Canonsburg Presbyterian Church responded to this call with initial gifts.

Through the years, MIPADEP continued to grow under the dynamic leadership of Principal Jean Bernard Saintimé. The school now enrolls more than 600 students annually. They travel miles, many of them walking, from such communities as Puron, Giraud, Fessard, Boutilliers, Pèlerin, Soisson La Montagne, and Fermathe. They are attracted by the expectation of a solid education offered at a very low tuition. In addition to salaries for teachers, we have supported the school by lending textbooks to students in the primary and secondary sections, donating books to students at the preschool level, and providing a daily hot lunch to everyone. Results at official examinations show high performance of MIPADEP students. Some years, the students have even reached 100 percent success.

MIPADEP students continue to excel in post-secondary studies and in professional performance. The school is currently run by Rose Marie Saint Fleury Louini, who serves as Pedagogical Director. She asserts that MIPADEP "is fully committed to the special mission — to transform the human being on the social and cultural level — and to help the community to grow intellectually (or, in more concrete terms, to enable it to develop all its dimensions and its potentialities, particularly at the socioeconomic level)."

One alumnus, Jacques-Nel Saint-Norable, expressed pride for his studies at MIPADEP — which is, in his estimation, a school aimed at the transformation of its students. Norable grew up in Thomassin. He states that MIPADEP represented his only path to an education. And he is very satisfied today saying, "I am a political science student at INAGHEL, the Institute of Political Science of the State University of Haiti. I am also the Director of Studies at Le Centre de Promotion de Competences Baptiste De Thomassin, a secondary school.All in all, I don't regret even a second of having been a student of the MIPADEP school. Excelsior! Ever Upward."

The Functional Literacy Ministry continues to make its mark in education in Haiti. It has helped in the training and professional careers of many. This impact is evident not only at MIPADEP, but also in the literacy campaign. From January 1983 to the present day, the Alliance d'Action Chretienne (AAC) has provided literacy skills to approximately 50,000 people in various parts of the country. It has enabled citizens to learn to read and write fluently and provided them with skills that guarantee their participation in both everyday life and in democratic activities in their respective communities.

CHAPTER 3
LOVE ALWAYS SERVES:
THE FLM BOARD

I was teaching at South High School on the South Side of Pittsburgh in the early 1980s when I met Martha Domske from Washington, Pennsylvania. She was a dedicated woman who worked as a practical nurse and aide at Western State School and Hospital for a decade to raise her five boys. As her oldest son approached college, she got the idea to go to college herself, and began to take courses at California State Teachers College in Western Pennsylvania. In 1969, Domske graduated from California State with a degree in special education. She was 38 when she began a 29-year career as a special ed teacher at South High School, eventually rising to head the Special Education Department.

She and I soon enjoyed a good relationship as colleagues. This relationship was greatly strengthened when we discovered the common ties that bound us in Christ. That bond opened the door for me to share with her my dreams for a better Haiti. She was the very first person, beside my wife Rozelle, whom I decided to approach with this idea. It happened once in our conversation when I explained to her the dire need for literacy in Haiti. With much compassion, she readily embraced the idea of a program addressing this issue. She also gave a resounding yes, expressing willingness to become active in such a project. Thus, she became one of the founding members of the board of FLM Haiti. She served for 25 years as secretary of the board. Martha Domske epitomized the solid commitment that became manifest with FLM Haiti board members.

EMBRACING FLM AS A FAITH JOURNEY

FLM Haiti took off thanks to the effort of a board of directors who (like Martha Domske) shared high levels of commitment! Vince Lombardi (the inspirational coach who during the 1960s led his Green Bay Packers team to six divisional titles, five National Championships and the first two Super Bowls), once advised, "Build for your team a feeling of oneness, of dependence on one another and of strength to be derived by unity." Step by step, the FLM board has succeeded in building, along these guidelines, a viable and meaningful organization driven by unity. It's a board coalesced into a dedicated team of committed individuals driven by a faith for change in Haiti. In my introductory monthly reports, delivered at each board meeting, I have always highlighted that "we live by faith, not by sight" (2 Corinthians 5:7, NIV). While the world advocates that seeing is believing, we stand unwaveringly on the conviction that "believing is seeing."

FLM board in the early days: Carol Williams, Bernadette Holmes and daughter Farah Holmes, Martha Domske, Sheila Archie, Marlene Branson, guest Pastor Joseph Simon, Sanford Chisholm, Dr. Beryl Jackson, with Dr. Leon Pamphile

The FLM Haiti Board has also been strongly guided by the spirit of unselfish love. At each board meeting, I consistently underscore that "love never fails." The power of love is strongly rooted in the belief that "love does not seek its own." The only rationalization behind our adventures in Haiti with FLM is that the person who loves is not bound by his/her own interests. The power of love has carried us beyond the goals of personal gain and worldly honor.

When I consider the amount of time, energy, and resources invested in this organization over the years, I realize that this undertaking would have been impossible had it been driven by any motto other than the altruistic desire to serve and help our fellow brothers and sisters. Theologian and Professor A. Van Ruler said most appropriately, "The way of the Gospel (which) leads us to integrate ourselves into the world is the way of self-denial. Only as we seek not ourselves but give ourselves to other men, and only as we seek not our own things but give ourselves to the things of others, do we really discover the world and our neighbor and, miraculously, only do we discover ourselves.Only then, indeed, have we really found God.He who loses his life shall find it." Board members and friends of FLM have been consistently driven by the tenets of the power of love to continue to do good.

Alongside board members such as Martha Domske, FLM was blessed in its earlier days to have another staunch servant in the person of Dr. Beryl Haughton Jackson, who chaired the board for two decades. Jackson was born in Cambridge, Jamaica and as a child dreamed of being a nurse. But after her mother's death, she put aside her studies until she was 27 years old to help raise her siblings. Considered too old for Jamaican nursing schools, she moved to England where she studied at Hackney Hospital in London. She later went to Canada, where she practiced as a nurse-midwife for six years.

She moved to Pittsburgh to marry McIver Jackson

Martha Domske, FLM founding member and first FLM secretary, who served for 25 years

and continued her education — earning a bachelor's degree in nursing at Duquesne University in 1970, then going on to earn a master's degree in 1972, and a doctoral degree in 1982 at the University of Pittsburgh. She became a clinician in psychiatric-mental health nursing, working with middle-aged African American women in Pittsburgh's Upper Hill District as a group psychotherapist. Recognized as an expert in her field, she was internationally known for her study, "Life Satisfaction in Black Climacteric Women in Relation to Specific Life Events." Jackson's contributions to nursing were acknowledged in 1991 with the Honorary Recognition Award of the Pennsylvania Nurses Association. In 1996, she received the Pitt School of Nursing Distinguished Alumni Award.

As she excelled in academia, Jackson still found time to chair the board of the Functional Literacy Ministry. A strong woman of faith, she usually opened our meetings with a very inspiring devotion. Emphasizing the power of faith and patience, she stated that it is better to "wait and be still, rather than forging blindly ahead." She would continue on, highlighting the words of Moses to the people of Israel and emphasizing God's companionship with our board.

Jackson was also a woman of prayer. She carried in her purse a small notebook in which she kept the names of the people and various causes she committed in prayer before the Lord. FLM occupied a special place in that notebook, as she always upheld the ministry and God's people in Haiti in prayer. As the situation in Haiti was most often punctuated by political instability and natural disasters, Chairwoman Jackson reminded us that we wouldn't always be in a mountaintop experience, and there was a reward for going through trials. As she put it, "Hidden under the work of trials is a blessing." She prayed for showers of blessings to pour on FLM's works and the people of Haiti. Inspired by the great faith the Lord bestowed in her over her long and productive trajectory, she kept the board rooted in commitment to the Lord and to the work. She upheld before us the fact that we were blessed because we belong to the family of God.

Among her many contributions, Jackson helped design the philosophy of the organization to align with Judeo-Christian traditions — to minister to the whole person as body, mind, and soul. She emphasized that we rely on God for the ongoing provision of the ministry. She was a servant leader who used her foresight to bring to our meetings practical ideas to keep our ministry in the right orbit of growth, and she sought ways to provide greater and better service to the poor and needy in Haiti.

Dr. Jackson worked especially hard to make our annual banquet a success by inviting friends from her church and the community, along with her colleagues from the University of Pittsburgh. Through Jackson,

Dr. Beryl Jackson

Dr. Joyce Penrose, also a professor of nursing at the University of Pittsburgh, became a superb worker in the ranks of FLM. (Penrose made several trips to Haiti and chaired a health committee to support the work.) Besides giving of her talents and time, Jackson also gave her money to support our annual banquet and to buy Bibles for literacy graduates in Haiti.

WORKING WITH GOD

"Commit your works to the Lord and your plans will succeed" (Proverbs 16:3, AMP).

Since the beginning, the FLM Board has been persuaded that we are working with God, who would always bring more success to our endeavors. In his book, *The Rhythm of Life*, Richard Exley says: "We are working with him to feed, clothe and shelter his human family. We share his dream for a world where poverty, disease, injustice and unrighteousness have been obliterated. He is the eternal architect; we are just the cement mixers. Still, there's something grand about working with HIM."

Working with God has helped the FLM board realize our dependence on Him for every need of the ministry. As we lean on God, He gives us new ideas to advance the ministry. In October 1986, as funds were slow in coming to push the work forward, the Lord inspired me to write a monthly sermon that was passed to churches and friends for a donation of 50 cents as a contribution to FLM. For a number of years, I applied myself faithfully to this task. Under the theme of "strength to overcome," every month board members brought contributions resulting from proceeds of this sermon. The sermon became an effective and relevant tool to promote the ministry. There were testimonies that people were blessed through these messages.

The sermons were shared not only in churches but also in hospitals. They were also mailed to contributors and friends. These blessings were nothing but a confirmation of hymn writer William Cowper's testimony about God's wonders. As he put it, "God moves in mysterious ways, His wonders to perform. He plants his footsteps in the sea and rides upon the storm." The story of FLM is a story of how God moves in mysterious ways in the life of this organization.

THE WORKING BOARD

The expression "working board" was used in my executive report on November 8, 1984. Indeed, from the outset, board members contributed faithfully to make this organization a reality, contributing time and resources to help FLM achieve its mission. In this spirit, they have assumed the role of a working board by various ways and means. Over the years, board members have provided financial resources as well as benevolent service. Board members are also fervent advocates of the cause.

As early as 1984, board member Sheila Archie had her pastor invite me, as FLM's Executive Director, to speak. She went to churches and other organizations, and made slide presentations of the newly-born FLM program. Then there was Marlene Branson, an English teacher in the Pittsburgh public schools, who played a great role as a treasurer and public relations figure for FLM. She coordinated several activities and helped publish our very first newsletter. Branson later moved on and became interested in genealogy. She co-authored a book with Bill Davidson in 2002, *Early African American Life in Waynesburg, Greene County, Pennsylvania.*

FLM fundraising event, sponsored by Jim and Carolyn Russ

Also, Carolyn Spicer Russ exemplifies well the concept of a working board. A native of Minnesota, Russ received her B.A. from the University of Minnesota. She served in the Peace Corps in Morocco, and later received her law degree in 1979 from the George Washington University in Washington, D.C. She devoted her practice to estate planning and meeting the legal needs of the elderly and the "Boomer" generation. After working for U.S. Steel's Public Affairs Department in Pittsburgh, Washington, D.C., and Chicago, she returned to Pittsburgh and opened her own practice. She became active in various civic and charitable organizations, particularly FLM Haiti.

Russ was also a copy editor of scholarly books. In 2001, The University Press of Florida gave her my manuscript, "Haitians and African Americans." She showed it to her neighbor, Florence Rouzier, a Haitian American who said that I lived in Pittsburgh. She noticed in my biography something about an organization called Functional Literacy Ministry of Haiti. As she puts it: "I was at an affair at my then-church, the Community of Reconciliation, and mentioned the book and the author. Whoever I was talking to knew and liked [Leon Pamphile]. I decided this whole sequence of events was a sign from God that I should offer my services to this organization." Russ joined the board in February 2003. She brought to the FLM board the kind of energy that took the organization to a new level of excellence. She had previously served on boards, and was even an executive director of a nonprofit organization. From these premises, she motivated the board to engage more in fundraising efforts.

She soon joined words to action. With her husband, Jim Russ, a professor of physics at Carnegie Mellon University, they hosted three "musical soirees" at their house. They invited two singers from their church, Carly Black and Gail Novak Mosites, accompanied by a few of Pittsburgh's finest accompanists, to put on a concert. Since their house wasn't terribly big, they cleared out all the furniture except for chairs. People sat on the floor at the singers' feet, on the stairway, in the kitchen, even on the porch. They prepared several kinds of soup, which encouraged everyone to meet in the kitchen as they tried the various kinds, including a Haitian soup made by my wife Rozelle. And desserts — wonderful desserts! Most of the people we met during the soirees are still on the FLM mailing list, still donating.

Over the years, Russ also served as FLM treasurer, edited the newsletter, and maintained the mailing list. She also helped with (and admired) the remarkable efforts of individuals such as Sue Robinson and Mary Gregg, who organized the mission trips — and Carol Williams, who contributed so much to so many efforts. She particularly grew to love the chair of the organization, Beryl Jackson, for her generosity and her commitment to prayer. Russ found the board to be the one place where she could be in community with African Americans and whites; liberal Christians and more conservative Christians; with different prayer styles and beliefs — in equal numbers with equal responsibilities. She cherished these relationships.

TEAMWORK

In Jim Collins' book, *From Good to Great*, offers a powerful strategy on the steps to build a great organization. To reach such a goal, Collins recommends having a "disciplined team with disciplined thought and with disciplined action." On this foundation, we can consistently reach out for a breakthrough. When we consider the evolution of FLM, it is awesome to realize that we have been blessed not only with a disciplined team but also an anointed team. It is a team coalesced around a common goal: HELP HAITIANS HELP THEMSELVES.

Not only a disciplined team, the FLM Haiti team has equally exemplified itself for its ability to thrive through teamwork. American poet Edgar Albert Guest helps us to fully appreciate the ultimate value of teamwork. In one of his poems, he states:

They may sound your praise and call you great,

They may single you out for fame,

But you must work with your running mate

Or you'll never win the game;

Oh, never the work of life is done

By the man with a selfish dream,

For the battle is lost or the battle is won

By the spirit of the team.

The Board of FLM Haiti has moved as a team to raise funds for the organization by holding two main annual activities: a concert in the spring and a fall banquet. Not only do these events bring funds for the ministry, but they also have served as a great promotional tool through the years. They've helped to keep the fire burning. They also make for a great opportunity to meet new people, increase fellowship and build givers. Our staple song for these events has been, "Thank you, Jesus, everything is going to be alright."

Our very first banquet took place on November 5, 1988, at Wilson, a banquet hall in the East Liberty neighborhood of Pittsburgh. In the years soon after, Elizabeth Bennett was always faithful in planning the banquet. For many years, she made arrangements for venues and planned menus. In later years, Carol Williams, who became chairperson of fundraising for FLM, took over the task of organizing our banquets. With many years of prayer and fasting, Williams also coordinated services to raise funds for the ministry. She made several mission trips to

Haiti along with her husband, Nate, and her daughter, Monaca.

She was so courageous. Even after dialysis became a regimen of her health care, it did not deter her from going to Haiti. Williams had me research and identify a dialysis treatment center in Port-au-Prince, Haiti's capital, not too far from where our ministry work was centered. When I located a site, she moved forward with her plan to go to Haiti.

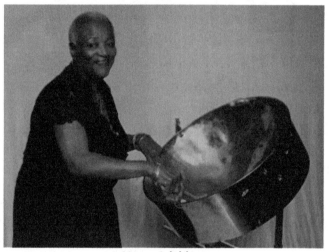

Verna Crichlow

FLM's banquet has always been fervently animated, thanks to Verna Crichlow and her Caribbean Vibes group. Crichlow came to America some 50 years ago from Trinidad and Tobago and raised her five kids mostly on her own. She retired as a math teacher from the Woodland Hills School District in 2004. Her Caribbean Vibes steel band originated as a family group, and as the demand for Caribbean culture became obvious and needed in the Pittsburgh community, its popularity grew. For 25 years, Crichlow has rocked her steel drums and her Caribbean vibes at our banquet, creating a highly festive atmosphere.

THE GIVING BOARD

At the 16th anniversary of FLM in 1999, I shared that nobody but God has kept the fire of this ministry burning within our hearts and the vision always shining before our eyes. This ministry was launched by faith; it has thus far stayed on course by faith; it will continue to thrive by faith. This faith was manifested, in great part, through the generous spirit of giving board members. They invested their financial resources, talents, and skills in the ministry. In the early years, Barbara Kunschner, a member of a United Methodist church, became a major donor and was the financial backbone of the ministry. For many years, she served as our treasurer. She gave from her personal resources and encouraged others to do the same. We received from Kunschner a generous donation of $10,000, which we used to establish as an investment fund — a rainy-day fund for the ministry.

As we moved forward, FLM's operation in Haiti was largely supported by a "giving board." On average, half of the monthly funds earmarked for the ministry was raised at board meetings. On February 8, 1997, board chairperson Beryl Jackson exhorted the board with scriptures from Leviticus, Psalms, and 1 John, reminding us of the principles of stewardship, where God informs us of His ownership of the earth's produce and instructs man to use it wisely for His glory. The board listened and acted on this message. Board members invested their talents in various ways to secure funds for the ministry.

Russell Bynum, a Pittsburgh communications and marketing professional, who currently serves as deputy executive director, also represents that spirit of giving and service on the board. Bynum became motivated about Haiti through his mother, Hazel Bynum, who first discovered Haiti when she went there on a cruise with her church. Russell further

**Barbara Kunschner provided funds to build
a community center in Haiti.**

learned about mission work in Haiti through an organization called Friends for Mission, established by
Christian minister and author Dr. Bennie Goodwin
and his wife, Mary, in the 1970s.

Bynum and I met at one of the Friends for
Mission banquets. While his mother stayed on the
board of Friends for Missions, she encouraged her son
to be a part of FLM Haiti. Being an educator herself,
she liked the focus on education and started coming to FLM's events with him, while encouraging
her entire family to support as well. As time went
on, Bynum joined the board of Functional Literacy
Ministry of Haiti in 1987.

Some time after joining the FLM Board, Bynum
went to Haiti on a mission trip. One life-changing observation for him was getting off the plane in Port-au-
Prince and seeing all the people, in an effort to raise
money, reaching to help him with his bags. After he
chose a person to help, many others continued to beg

him to let them assist him as well. Seeing the poverty and desperation made him angry. He vowed then to do whatever he could to improve conditions in Haiti when he returned to the United States. Bynum became the chair of the board in January 2004. Recently, he was elevated to the position of deputy executive director of the ministry. Russell has been the event planner for all of FLM's activities. He has also managed well to keep the organization in the media.

Another faithful servant and board member was Maggie Elizabeth Hill, whom I met in January 1971 at the Pittsburgh Theological Seminary. She was one of the first friends I made in Pittsburgh. She became endeared to me and my wife Rozelle. Beyond this friendship emerged her strong commitment to the people of Haiti.

Hill was born in Atlanta, Georgia. After the death of her mother, she relocated to Boston with her maternal grandmother. After studying at Barrington College in Rhode Island and Boston State College, she served as a teacher and reading specialist in the Boston schools. Hill became an FLM board member and practically traveled to Haiti with most medical and educational mission teams. She established FLM's Boston chapter in 2005. That same year, the group hosted its first fundraising luncheon — and Hill was strongly supported in this endeavor by Mother Mildred Taylor, who was the backbone, the encourager of FLM Haiti Boston. Hill often referred to Taylor as "the wind beneath our wings." But Mother Taylor herself made that confession, saying, "FLM is my passion."

Every two years, Hill hosted the Boston chapter banquet with the goal of raising $10,000. She never missed the mark, and here is how she did it: "My fundraising is year-round, 24/7. If you come to my house and ask me for water, I will say, 'One dollar, please; all proceeds go to FLM Haiti.'" Hill had traveled to Haiti so many times, she said she lost count. She became an icon of every medical and educational mission trip; and she, eventually, considered herself a Haitian.

ADVISORY BOARD

On April 12, 1986, FLM established an advisory board, which included among others: Dr. Robert Kelly of the Pittsburgh Theological Seminary, Dr. Karl Lewis of the University of Pittsburgh School of Engineering, and Dr. Myrven Caines, a Pittsburgh physician. In later years, Dr. Ronald Peters, a minister and professor with the Pittsburgh Theological Seminary, also joined. The advisory board made various suggestions, such as counseling FLM to: connect with the World Health Organization and the World Bank; to consider involvement with the Catholic Church in Haiti (which was pushing for literacy); and to query small foundations for support possibilities. The support of the advisory board was invaluable in the advancement and growth of the ministry.

PARTNERSHIP WITH OTHER ORGANIZATIONS

From its early days, FLM has sought to fulfill its mission through partnership with other organizations. Our first partnership was with Christian Literacy Associates in Pittsburgh. The field director for this organization was the Rev. Jack Kennedy, who made an effective contribution in the early years of FLM by going to Haiti to hold a training seminar for our literacy teachers.

Other organizations lent their support to the work. From the beginning, Cornerstone TV, the Pittsburgh-based Christian broadcasting network, has consistently enabled us to introduce the ministry to the community at large. As early as 1984, I made an appearance at the station, which enabled me to connect with Barbara Kunschner. She later contacted me to express interest in serving, and soon became a productive board member. Cornerstone has also supported us with donations toward the construction of our medical and dental clinic.

FLM also enjoyed a fruitful partnership with Churches In Action (CIA), a group of churches in Western New York that gets together for volunteer projects. For many years, CIA has provided funds to purchase Bibles for our literacy graduates. Some of their members have gone on mission trips in Haiti. In fact, the CIA coordinator, Howard Rich, said; "I have been in Haiti 5-6 times on CIA-sponsored mission trips. We worked with FLM to support the school, distribute water filters to the community/school families, and provide Bibles to graduates of the FLM adult literacy program. One of the advantages of going on multiple missions trips is we could get to know teachers, translators, and the children we were supporting. We had the opportunity to see first-hand what their needs were ... not what we in Hamburg, NY thought they needed." CIA's contributions to FLM have been tremendous.

FLM Haiti also received a tremendous boost from Dr. Ronald Peters when he became professor of Urban Ministry at Pittsburgh Theological Seminary in 1991. Peters soon distinguished himself by his energetic dynamism in the Pittsburgh religious community. He established the seminary's Metro-Urban Institute (MUI), using it to help church leaders and congregations adapt to an increasingly urbanized society. Peters reached out to us to establish a partnership with FLM Haiti in 1994. This partnership opened up the door of the seminary for our events: concerts, banquets, and press conferences. He summarized his appreciation of the FLM/MUI partnership in these words:

"I was blessed to serve on the FLM Advisory

Board in the 1990s. It was a divine gift to be involved in supporting FLM in this way. Moreover, this paved the way for my participation in educational, medical, and clergy-training mission trips to Haiti with people touched by Christ in Haiti, the United States, and elsewhere. Given today's too frequent challenges of fear, alienation, poverty, violence, disease, war, and all manner of spiritual dysfunction, it is a divine gift to be involved with FLM — part of God's movement in the world as 'balm' (Jeremiah 8:22) from sin, pain, and dysfunction; and toward love, justice, reconciliation, help, healing, hope, and life! The half hasn't been told ... all that God has done, is doing now, and will do tomorrow for Haiti and the world through our faith in FLM."

The FLM Haiti Board continues to keep the ministry on the path of progress. It has evolved into a special kind of family, strongly bonded around a common cause. Compelled by love, the board is focused on brightening the future of the ministry. We believe that the Lord will continue to bless this noble mission.

CHAPTER 4
LOVE ALWAYS HEALS: PROVIDING HEALTH CARE

"Love has hands to help others. It has feet
to hasten to the poor and needy. It has eyes
to see misery and want. It has ears to hear
the sighs and sorrows of men. This is what
love looks like." — Augustine

Health care stands as one of the major indicators
of Haiti's failure to provide basic services to its population. The Haitian healthcare system lacks adequate
staffing, supplies, and infrastructure to meet the
needs of the most remote and marginalized communities. There is a serious shortage of healthcare personnel. Hospitals are severely inadequate. There are
25 physicians and 11 nurses for every 100,000 people. Most rural areas have no access to health care,
making residents susceptible to otherwise treatable
diseases. Roughly three-fourths of Haitian households lack running water. Unsafe water, along with
unsanitary living conditions, contribute to the high
incidence of infectious diseases.

At an FLM Haiti board meeting on May 14, 1988,
the idea to widen the scope of the ministry to include
health care was discussed. Dr. Richard Pantalone, a
former Pittsburgh-area physician who once served as
a surgeon in Haiti, attended the meeting and helped
shape that vision. He expressed the desire to establish a permanent medical clinic in Laboule, one of
the rural mountain communities we serve, by using

a physician who might visit periodically. The discussion focused on exploring Haiti's medical facilities and system of healthcare operation in Haiti, and deciding on the best ways to make the first steps in order to create a clinic. Pantalone, who had first-hand experience with the Albert Schweitzer Hospital (the long-time medical campus established in Haiti's Lower Artibonite Valley) and its dispensaries, expressed willingness to assist in the drafting of a letter. It would be sent to foundations to seek support for FLM's expansion into health care. Pantalone enlisted the support of board member Barbara Kunschner in sending such letters of inquiry.

The construction of a medical and dental clinic was laid out as a long-term goal for FLM at the February 20, 1993 board meeting. By 1994, the design for the clinic was ready. We were then in quest of funds for the construction of the building. The first donation toward the construction of the clinic came in 1996 from Cornerstone TV through the advocacy of Dr. Mitchel Nickols, pastor of the Bible Way Church in New Kensington. It was a solid step toward reaching our goal.

The turning point for the idea of providing health care to the people of Haiti took place when Rev. David Robinson and his wife, Susan, of the Crossroads Presbyterian Church in Washington, Pennsylvania, attended our fall banquet at the East Liberty Presbyterian Church (Pittsburgh) in the fall of 1998. They came at the invitation of Martha Domske, a member of that church. After the close of the banquet, they patiently waited until the crowd thinned for the opportunity to chat with me.

When I approached them, there was a little small talk, and then David abruptly inquired, "Pastor Leon, what is your vision for FLM Haiti?" Without any hesitation, I passionately responded that the people needed medical care. I let him know that I wanted to put together a medical team to go to Haiti.

Rev. Robinson responded positively to this request. At the board meeting of November 13, 1999, it was announced that Rev. Robinson planned to go to Haiti in the summer of 2000 to work on the school building and to provide medical service. The project was placed before the Lord for a successful outcome.

OUR FIRST MEDICAL MISSION

In July 1997, Christina Richardson, Maggie Hill (from Boston), and Rose Ellen Pamphile (my eldest child) went to Haiti with me as the very first mission team from FLM. *Teena*, as we affectionately called Christina, was the first board member to go to Haiti. Upon her return, she reported to the board that her "outstanding perception was the positive attitude exhibited by the Haitian people and their appreciation of being able to write their own names as a result of the FLM literacy program." With David Robinson on board, FLM mission teams to Haiti were ready to take on a new level of ministry.

House of David Medical Clinic

Our first full-scale summer medical mission got underway in July 2000. Rev. Robinson exhibited the leadership of a great organizer. His love for God and for people shone through the training of the first team he recruited to serve on that mission. That trip consisted of two pastors, a registered nurse, two medical aides, and a couple of physicians — Dr. Martin McCann and Dr. Sandra McCann.

In the preparatory meetings held at Crossroads Presbyterian Church, Rev. Robinson asked the team to memorize two passages of Scriptures before the trip. The first one was Philippians 2:3-4 (NIV): "Do nothing out of selfish ambition or vain conceit. Rather, in humility value others above yourselves, not looking to your own interests but each of you to the interests of the others." The second passage was 1 Thessalonians 2:8 (NIV): "We loved you so much, we were delighted to share with you not only the gospel of God but our lives as well." These two passages have remained the guiding light of our medical mission to this day. Rev. Robinson exhibited the mind of Christ as he served those who are less fortunate.

The spiritual training was soon followed by our first packing party for Haiti at Crossroads Presbyterian Church. A crowd of volunteers gathered to organize and pack stocks of supplies: medications, glasses, and school items. These supplies were checked, sorted, and placed in duffle bags to be transported to Haiti. Each team member was to bring two bags of 70 pounds each. All personal items were to be put in a carry-on.

On July 3, 2000, our first medical mission trip got underway. We were welcomed at the Toussaint Louverture International Airport of Port-au-Prince by a heavy downpour. And it rained cats and dogs the whole time we were there. I watched with apprehension as Rev. Robinson and team members climbed hills to reach the site for some of our mobile clinics. It was a vivid illustration of God's love in

House of David examination room

action. Medical service was provided to more than 1,000 Haitians during seven days. There were many cases of hypertension, vision maladies, stomach acid, etc. Children were severely affected with skin diseases and scabies. We dispensed medicine, vitamins, glasses, and hygiene kits. We left extra medicine for a public medical center in Port-au-Prince under the direction of Dr. Danielle Morisset, a devoted Haitian physician who attended to the health care of the needy in Bel-Air, a slum in Haiti's capital city.

The group attended the graduation exercises for the literacy program, where 157 young people and adults received certificates. Their excitement was evident and contagious. We also attended the end-of-the-year report cards exercise for our school. It was exciting to observe 350 young boys and girls proudly singing the national anthem, saluting their flag, and reciting the 23rd Psalm.

Rev. Robinson's wife, Susan, said that her husband had kept a journal while in Haiti and often shared some of his post-trip reflections with her: "At home he shared story after story about his experiences. He

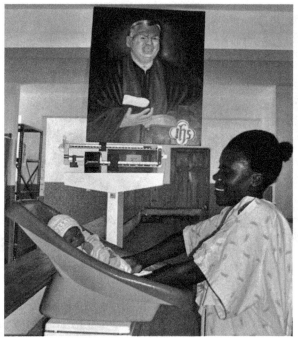

House of David pharmacy

talked about the huge numbers of people who came to the clinic each day. Close to a hundred people would be lined up outside the makeshift clinic early in the morning when the medical team arrived. They ranged from newborn babies to patients who were in their 90s. David wrote and shared with me the difference that an on-site clinic would make to the health and welfare of the people in villages in the surrounding area. David was a changed person when he returned home; he was so deeply moved by his experience, seeing poverty and desperate need firsthand."

Martha Domske was a member of that first medical mission trip. She saw the service provided in Haiti on the Fourth of July as "a Unique Independence Day." Riding from the school to the hotel after serving all day, she wrote, "We cheered loudly and burst into song. We harmonized on every patriotic song we could pull up from diverse memories, including our national anthem, Battle Hymn of the Republic, God Bless

America, and even Yankee Doodle Dandy. We were a triumphant group, to say the least, as we entered the hotel."

Success begets success. The next year, the dates of July 25 to August 2001 were set for the next trip to Haiti to administer health clinics. A film to be used for fundraising was completed at Waynesburg College, and a three-year plan for extensive fundraising was formulated. This time, Susan Robinson would be coming along. She commented: "I felt if our marriage was going to stay strong, I, too, wanted to experience the life-changing encounter [my husband] had. Since then, I have tried to visit Haiti twice a year."

During the second mission trip, Rev. Robinson soon realized that something more permanent needed to be done to meet the medical needs of the people of Thomassin, Laboule, Boutilliers, Kenscoff, and surrounding areas. He conveyed this message to the members of the team in the following words: "Much more needs to be accomplished so we can reach our goal of a permanent clinic run by Haitians, supported by FLM, and a support staff of doctors and nurses from the United States. We will also begin fundraising for the clinic and hopefully get a storage facility constructed at the Laboule school so we can begin shipping supplies there. Please be in prayer concerning these things." Rev. Robinson raised the funds that built the storage facility. When he moved to the area of Buffalo, New York, one of his first acts was to bring the plight of Haiti to the attention of the area ministers. Their churches gave the initial funds to begin the construction of the cistern for the clinic.

ADVENTURES

Nicki Perfetti first learned of FLM when she was working as a case manager for CompServices. Her boss, Carol Seckinger, learned of Perfetti's interest in going on a medical mission trip and directed

Perfetti to FLM (because her husband, Dr. Richard Seckinger, just happened to be the mentor for my doctoral dissertation at the University of Pittsburgh). In 2001, Perfetti went to Haiti on her first mission trip and later joined the board. She became very active in planning and fundraising. In 2003, she raised funds for the construction of the clinic. Perfetti shared that our medical missions were at times punctuated with adventures. Anticipating such occurrences, I encouraged every potential volunteer to apply a key principle: "MONITOR AND ADJUST."

Perfetti described one of these adventures, which took place in Boutilliers, one of the mountain communities where we provide aid: "We served a large group of Haitians in a church high in the mountains. The church was very difficult to reach, and we had to literally climb the hill to get to it. During our time at the church, there was a very bad storm that lasted several hours. After it stopped, we as a team now had to descend from the mountain.

"I remember us literally sliding down the mountain on cardboard, passing Haitians with their animals on the way. After we arrived at our van (several hours after we were to depart), we drove not very far from the site when we encountered a road that had been blocked. A very large tower had fallen during the storm. So here we were again, having to "Monitor and Adjust," as Leon always said. We got to the van and started to move the debris. Through the grace of God, and Haitians appearing out of the brush to help, we eventually arrived back at the hotel close to 8 p.m."

PLANS TO BUILD THE CLINIC

From the very beginning of our mission trips to Haiti, we have identified high blood pressure as a major health problem facing the population. Pharmacist Lynn Moran, a stalwart and longtime supporter, described it in these terms: "The most pervasive health issue we found among our Haitian brothers and sisters was hypertension — 220/190, 190/170, 210/165 — to mention a few common combinations. We would often retake the blood pressures, thinking that the information handed to us on the patient records and on the prescriptions for blood pressure medications had to be a mistake. However, after the nurses on our team rechecked many of these, we quickly learned that the Haitian people had a huge struggle to keep their blood pressure normal and manageable. They needed treatment. We would often ask ourselves, 'Did we bring enough blood pressure medication to treat all of these folks until our return? Was this alone the answer?' We discovered after our first couple of trips, it was not. We needed blood pressure education, and we needed medication to be purchased ongoing from a Haitian supplier."

House of David patient care

This serious predicament was at the root of a plan to build a clinic in the Thomassin community. Originally, the clinic property had been acquired right in front of the Thomassin church, not too far from our school. But in February 2004, Rozelle and I decided to donate our recently acquired adjacent property. It was a much larger site on which to build the clinic.

It was decided that the original site would be used to build a technical school. Rev. David Robinson remained at the forefront of the project. In early 2003 when he moved to Hamburg Presbyterian Church in western New York, he engaged the congregation there in fundraising. An anonymous donor from his church made a substantial contribution toward the construction of the clinic. By June 2003, this amount increased because of the generosity of a consortium of churches in Buffalo, New York, to fund a cistern under the clinic for water provision.

A breakthrough in that process came when Ben Roberts, the son of Dr. Sam Roberts, raised the possibility of networking with the Building Goodness Foundation (BGF) of Charlottesville, Virginia, to support the effort. Dr Sam Roberts was a well-known physician in the town of Elkins, West Virginia. Before FLM came to know him, he had been involved in northern Haiti, where he built a clinic. Rev. David Robinson recruited him to join the FLM medical team, and his contribution was invaluable.

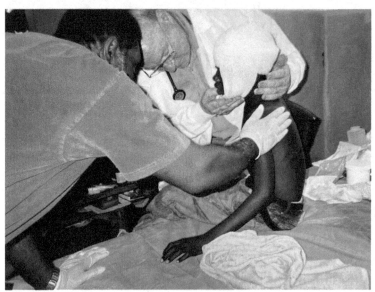

Dr. Sam Roberts attending to a boy with third-degree burns

When Dr. Sam Roberts contacted BGF, the group pledged to help build the clinic and to support us in fundraising and transportation of materials as well. In July 2004, architects Enoch Snyder and Steve Davis of BGF went to Haiti to gather information to design the community health center. They also met with Haitian volunteers who would work with BGF.

Dr. Roberts further organized an encounter between FLM and representatives of the Building Goodness Foundation (BGF). On August 28, 2004, Susan Robinson, Nicki Perfetti, and I traveled to Elkins, West Virginia to meet with Dr. Roberts, and the architects Snyder and Davis. They shared with us the designs for the community health center. Two representatives were scheduled to go to Haiti for further exploration in building the foundation.

HOW DO YOU BUILD A CLINIC IN HAITI?

Reflecting on the process of building the clinic, Susan Robinson saw God's hand in the whole thing. "People started to pray, and God began to draw us together. Through the special talents and abilities of so many, He transformed a simple cornfield into the vision all believed in. He used people from the local Haitian community, and people from all across the United States."

The Haitian community responded with much enthusiasm to the construction project. Some 200 people showed up for the groundbreaking ceremony. For the construction work, BGF sent various teams. After many efforts were hindered by political instability in Haiti, progress was eventually made in the construction of the community health center. In June 2007, though still unfinished, the medical mission was held for the first time in the building. "It was so exciting to walk into the clinic, greet the people, and see all the work that has been accomplished. The building was enclosed, and all walls were up," Susan Robinson recalled. "On the first floor there were nine rooms. I was overwhelmed with emotion as I walked from room to room taking it all in."

House of David patient registration

It was a great advance. The work on the clinic made it possible to hold much-needed classes, especially in the area of hygiene. It also made possible the establishment of a pilot project to treat high blood pressure on an ongoing basis. Fifty patients were selected and started on medication. Their pressure would be monitored once a month by a trained Haitian clinician, who would email the results to Dr. Joby Joseph (a physician in West Virginia) and Donald Robinson (a physician from Hamburg, New York), who would monitor care via computer.

DEDICATION OF THE HOUSE OF DAVID

The clinic was inaugurated on July 4, 2009. Its opening was attended by more than 100 people, mainly local Haitians and U.S. missionary workers. The chairman of our board of directors, Russell Bynum, was also in attendance. The setting was well decorated and enhanced with lively music. A repast followed the dedication ceremony. At the dedication service, the new director, Esdras Germain, underscored the importance of the clinic for the community. As he stated, the Haitian government does not have the political will to provide medical care for the population. For rural residents, this is especially challenging because they live even farther from any medical facilities.

With the inauguration of the House of David, residents now had a facility close to them. Additionally, FLM would use young professionals in the community to work as doctors, dentists, nurses, and a manager of the clinic. The benefit of this project for the community was tremendous.

Beginning construction of the House of David Medical Clinic

Sue Robinson was very appreciative of this accomplishment and knew of its potential to strengthen, educate, and heal local people. She commented: "Because we have the space and a talented young mission volunteer, we held small classes consisting of five to seven Haitian women at a time to teach about hygiene. Their response was so positive! In our planning for the clinic, teaching about health has always been one of the major goals, and this was our first opportunity to try it."

After a decade of prayers and hard work, the House of David was finally opened to the public. As it began to get established and organized, FLM was thankful for the selfless service of Kate Tomlinson. Ms. Tomlinson went to Haiti as a member of one of our medical mission teams. She returned with much fervor to advance the cause. Soon she joined the FLM board and helped to set up the first FLM website.

Reverend David Robinson, pictured with his wife, Susan Robinson, initiated medical mission trips to Haiti.

In helping with the House of David, Tomlison was instrumental in reaching out to Global Links — a nonprofit source of hospital supplies and a limited source of primary care supplies. He persuaded the group to agree to supply equipment for the clinic. In addition, the Hamburg Presbyterian mission board voted unanimously to give $15,000 to enable Global Links to transport the material. As a result, the clinic was equipped with exam tables, chairs, desks, a dental exam chair, filing cabinets, a microscope, computer, scales, and much more. The clinic was named House of David, in honor of Rev. David Robinson, who ignited the project.

ONGOING MEDICAL MISSION

Medical mission trips, which started in 2000 under the dynamic leadership of Rev. David Robinson, continued to advance by leaps and bounds. During the summer trip of 2001, 14 health workers went and provided care for some 1,250 people during seven clinic sessions. The summer medical mission of 2003 grew larger. We had 19 participants, who transported 33 duffle bags, each weighing 70 pounds, with an estimated value of $50,000. Mary Gregg, a Pittsburgh-area businesswoman, became coordinator of the summer medical mission and worked with such nonprofit groups as Operation Blessing, King Benevolent Fund, and MAP International to secure these supplies. She coordinated packings that attracted significant press coverage for mission trips.

Our health workers touched the lives of 1,100 Haitians who needed medical care and vision services. The team was a victim of its own success. When word got around regarding the good service provided, we were practically mobbed the following day. On the last clinic day, some 600 Haitians showed up. This number overwhelmed us, forcing us to cancel services that day.

The success of our medical mission grew even stronger in 2005 when we had the largest mission team to date. Volunteers came from New York, Boston, Pittsburgh, Philadelphia, and Elkins, West Virginia. The travelers carried 35 bags, each weighing 70 pounds, stuffed with medicines, vitamins, eyeglasses, educational kits, caps, and t-shirts. These American missionaries were joined by four Haitian local physicians, 14 interpreters and helpers, and 25 teachers from two schools.

More than 2,000 patients were seen. Eyeglasses were issued to more than 500 people. Thirty minor surgeries took place. A young woman, Gladys, who had experienced a severe burn, was cared for — and an 8-month-old infant, diagnosed with severe malnutrition and dehydration — was placed in a local orphanage for care following treatment. Evangelism was an added dimension to this year's activities.

Maggie Hill, founder of the Boston chapter of FLM Haiti

The physicians attending our mission trips did their very best to provide care beyond the medical capacities available in Haiti. In 2001, one of them observed that the main physical condition plaguing the Haitians, especially the children, was malnutrition and intestinal parasites. The children who came, some with their mothers and some alone, had no body mass, no muscle elasticity or reflexes, and were underdeveloped in size and weight because of improper nutrition.

Beyond malnutrition, two cases caused our physicians to consider finding treatment for Haitian children in the United States. One little girl was diagnosed with hydrocephalus by Dr. Charles Tripoli of Washington, Pennsylvania. It had such a profound effect on the doctor that he led an effort arranging for the child to be flown to Pittsburgh for treatment at Children's Hospital. Dr. Martin McCann, another one of our physicians, a pathologist from Washington, D.C., examined a young boy with a severe cleft lip. Dr. McCann searched the Internet for surgeons who might come to Haiti to perform facial surgery.

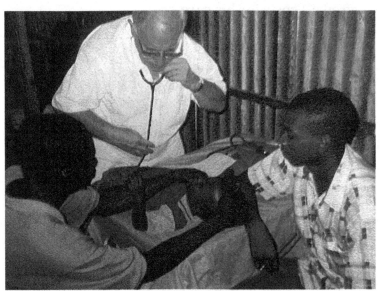

Dr. Charles Tripoli at the first medical mission in 2000

Such outreach did not always have a successful outcome. However, there is one story that shines through. Randy was brought to the United States for treatment in 2006. Because of malnutrition, he was a 12-year-old boy who was only about the size of an 8-year-old. His head had been burned by boiling oil. He was treated once, but inappropriately. He was infected, and the burn covered half of the surface of his head.

Providentially, Dr. Sam Roberts had brought along medicine and dressing material to attend to such a case. He sedated Randy and treated him with antibiotics. Then he drained the wound, cleaned it, and wrapped it. With the help of Dixie Bickel, the head of an orphanage in the local Haitian community, an arrangement was made to fly Randy to the United States for a skin graft. He was able to go to the Shriners Hospital for Children for treatment in December 2006. His graft was successful. We gave God praise for answered prayers. He lived with a host family before returning to Haiti — and a year later, he returned to Shriners Hospital for hair treatment. The hospital covered all costs for his care.

Young boy with third-degree burns following treatment

Young boy with third-degree burns — making progress

**Young boy with third-degree burns in Boston,
after receiving treatment at Shriner's Hospital in Boston, MA**

WINTER MEDICAL MISSION

From 2000 on, the medical mission became a summer event. As interest in medical mission trips increased more and more, a winter medical mission trip was added in January 2008. A team of 10 workers, joined by two Haitian doctors and six translators, provided care for about 400 people. The doctors discovered two cases of cancer. We urged the two patients to seek further medical care. It was during one of these mission trips that Melody Loudin, a nurse from West Virginia, described what she witnessed as "an ordinary procedure with miraculous results."

In her words, "A desperate mother brought her baby to this year's clinic. When the baby arrived, she was severely dehydrated and on the verge of death. The medical team administered a glucose gel, then gave the girl saline solution and Pedialyte with a dropper until she recovered. After she was stable, the team treated her for an infection. God truly works miracles through our medical members."

Our missionary physicians also identified additional health needs in the community that were not being met as well as they could be. They observed, for instance, many unaddressed pediatric problems. There were children with low weight, anemia, malnutrition, and congenital heart diseases, along with high rates of respiratory infections and diarrhea. They determined that having a pediatrician on staff would mean that FLM could better respond to the needs of the children — and shape better outcomes for everyone, from newborns to those in early adolescence. As a result, in the spring of 2014, a Haitian pediatrician was hired. Adding this valuable service made a positive impact on the health of the children in the community.

During the medical mission in January 2016, Dr. Robin McGuire made a commitment to initiate a gynecological program at the clinic. As she stated, "I have traveled to Haiti for many years. On the first mission to Haiti, I had been surprised by the number of women who said that they personally knew of a woman who died during childbirth. Many patients discussed their experience of sisters, cousins, and friends dying during childbirth. The maternal mortality rate in Haiti is the highest in the western hemisphere. These women also spoke of stillbirth, neonatal death, and the loss of children. I was also surprised by the enormous number of women with chronic hypertension and pre-eclampsia. I took a survey of the pregnant women who came to the clinic and the antenatal care they had received. The results were staggering. This prompted me to begin a dialogue with FLM Haiti regarding the addition of an obstetrician to the clinic's team of physicians." As a result of Dr. McGuire's effort, a gynecologist was added to our medical staff to meet the needs of women's care.

The service provided to the various communities we serve in Haiti was greatly enhanced with the support of Dr. Bill Markle and his wife, Mary. Dr. Markle was on the staff of the University of Pittsburgh Medical School when I met with him in 2003. We began a discussion about the possible involvement of Pitt medical students in our medical mission trips to Haiti. Dr. Markle felt students could go in January, since June is such a busy time. He shared our current need with his colleagues — and as a result, Dr. Madeline Simasek, a pediatrician, joined the team.

Dr. Markle relates how he became involved with FLM: "I had been involved with a healthcare project in Honduras for some time when Leon Pamphile approached me about helping with a fairly new medical work in Haiti. I had enough on my plate at the time and was not particularly interested, but, as you know Leon is very persistent and persuasive. As I learned more about FLM and its commitment to helping better all aspects of the lives of people in the Thomassin and Kenscoff regions of Haiti, I became more interested. Also, Leon's enthusiasm and dedication made both my wife, Mary, and I more willing, and even eager, to help in whatever way we could."

As director of the family medicine clerkship at the University of Pittsburgh Medical School, Dr. Markle would regularly bring students with him to help. He emphasized this practice, saying, "The experience also gave them some exposure to the health problems in Haiti and other resource-poor locations. With time, I began to bring family medicine and internal medicine residents, and they always felt the experience was a highlight of their education. A few times, we needed to have the students take their clerkship examination in Haiti. We did an OSCE (Objective Structured Clinical Examination) in Haiti using the volunteer staff as 'patients.' All the students passed this exam.

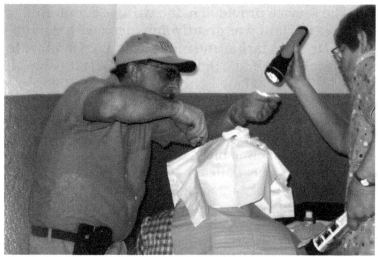

Dr. William Markle and his wife, Mary Markle, providing care to patients in Haiti

"Some of them even returned to Haiti a second time. Although I was primarily in charge of them, every medical professional on the team functioned as their teacher. This now included Dr. Dieudonne Catulle, the Haitian physician who had been hired to run the clinic during the times an American team was not there — which was most of the year."

The clinic continues to provide good service to the community. I remember well during one of my morning walks how humbling it was to see the line forming at the gate as early as 7 a.m., a full hour before the normal 8 a.m. opening. It was a sign of appreciation from the patients who received service there. Dr. Dieudonne Catulle, who has been serving as physician and is currently the medical director of the center, understands the impact of the clinic (perhaps more so than others).

Dr. Catulle told me: "Since the opening of the center in 2009, we have had 35,602 patients visiting the institution for medical consultations, despite a limited number of staff. But with the unparalleled dedication of the staff, we have worked diligently to meet our objective, which is to satisfy the community served."

She further added that the clinic allows the area's residents and the larger community to benefit from having the best health care nearby, because not having to travel long distances eliminates one of the obstacles to accessing health care. Women of child-bearing age benefit from appropriate gynecological care, and pregnant women benefit from prenatal follow-up care, up to eight-and-a-half months into their pregnancy. Above all, the clinic enables people in the community to better understand their illness and trust the care because it provides established and evidence-based medical treatment. "Because of poverty and political instability, people were truly burdened and prevented from receiving proper care," she says. FLM is always part of the solution.

FLM Haiti theme song

Leon (front) and David coming down from the mountain after a full day at the medical clinic in Boutilliers

CHAPTER 5
LOVE ALWAYS PERSEVERES: COPING WITH DISASTER IN HAITI

THE HORRIFIC EARTHQUAKE OF JANUARY 12, 2010

The year 2010 began like business as usual for FLM. On the morning of January 9, we had our regular board meeting. We welcomed the 27th anniversary of FLM's service to the Haitian people. We rejoiced over what was so far an exciting journey. We were getting ready for the Winter Medical and Education mission trip. A strong team of 26 participants was all set to depart for Haiti. We had established a different focus this time, by planning to have physicals for all of the 600 students at our school. We had water filters for teachers and students at the school.

All these plans were shattered three days later on January 12, 2010 when a large-scale earthquake struck the country. The initial shock registered a magnitude of 7.0, and was soon followed by two aftershocks of magnitudes 5.9 and 5.5. More aftershocks occurred in the following days, including another one of magnitude 5.9 that struck on January 20 at Petit Goâve, a town some 35 miles (55 km) west of Port-au-Prince. An exact death toll proved elusive. The Haitian government's official count was more than 300,000, which would make the earthquake's aftermath one of the worst natural disasters in recorded history, but other estimates were considerably smaller. Hundreds of thousands of survivors were displaced.

Haiti was a country in ruins. The collapsed buildings that defined the landscape of the disaster area came as a consequence of Haiti's lack of building codes. Without adequate reinforcement, the buildings disintegrated under the force of the quake, killing or trapping their occupants. In Port-au-Prince, the Notre Dame Cathedral and the National Palace were both heavily damaged.

The earthquake also caused serious damage in the community of Thomassin, where we serve. Hard hit there were the poor, whose homes and workplaces were not securely built. It is estimated that 30,000 government and commercial buildings collapsed, and some 250,000 homes were destroyed.

People without shelter need homes

January 13, 2010, the day after the earthquake, remained an unforgettable day for me. In the ensuing chaos, there was a widespread mobilization to rescue and provide relief for Haitians. I remember sitting in my living room with a writing pad in my right hand and the phone on my left ear. People across the United States, in a sudden wave of goodwill, reached out to me to inquire how they could help. Among the callers was Kelly Eplee, the Executive Director of Building Goodness Foundation (BGF) — the Charlottesville, Virginia organization that had helped build the FLM Community Health Center in Thomassin. He expressed BGF's commitment to help with the relief and reconstruction effort in Haiti.

INITIAL RESPONSE TO THE EARTHQUAKE

FLM's board members went on the offensive. Russell Bynum, our board chair, upon seeing the devastation of this horrific earthquake, felt the need to do something. He recalled taking this action: "I called those in the media whom I knew had received many news releases and calls about our banquets. They agreed to allow Bishop Pamphile, Luke Hingson of Brother's Brother Foundation, and myself to come and talk about the earthquake and conditions in Haiti. Newscasters like Lynne Hayes-Freeland, Chris Moore, Jon Delano, Jonas Chaney, and many in the media (both local and national) interviewed Dr. Pamphile and others. *The Pittsburgh Post-Gazette* and other publications listed FLM as *one of the groups to donate to* for earthquake relief," Russell explained.

My wife, Kathy, and I run a communications firm called Bynums Marketing & Communications, Inc. Our clients came to our aid and helped us do a fundraiser in Mount Washington at the house of Attorney Donald Kortlandt and his wife, Anna Singer. The first year was a tremendous success, and the funding was used to support the building of the Excelsior Technical Institute."

Another board member, Carolyn Russ, also rushed into action to help Haiti. Upon learning that larger organizations in the city were using the earthquake as a fundraising opportunity, Russ, as she recalled, "immediately drafted a letter for Leon's signature, printed out the letter and labels, and got a mailing out to our ever-generous, kind supporters within two days of the earthquake. The contributions started coming in that very week. The letter raised more than $100,000. To God be the glory. Seriously."

Russell Bynum

Carolyn Russ, FLM board member, who transformed the administrative practices of the ministry

After the earthquake, FLM was propelled from an organization that raised a few hundred dollars a month to send to Haiti (to help in the area of education) to an organization that employed more than 100 employees in Haiti with a K-13 school, a health clinic, a trade school, a mission residence, and more than 50 reading centers.

EXPANDING THE FLM/BGF PARTNERSHIP

Overnight the partnership between FLM and BGF was reinforced as both organizations joined hands to respond to the crisis. The two nonprofits quickly formed a platform for rebuilding. In 2010, BGF was barely 10 years old, and Kelly Eplee had been its new executive director for only a few months. The relationship between FLM and BGF was not new, but the earthquake fused the organizations and pushed them both to new heights of service, accomplishing things barely imaginable before that time. Little did we know how many thousands of lives would receive vital education, shelter, and capacity from the FLM/BGF partnership.

Jack Horn with Building Goodness Foundation workers in Haiti

Since all commercial flights to Haiti came to a halt, something miraculous took place. Through a BGF contact, an anonymous donor made available his private jet to take an FLM and BGF team to Port-au-Prince. Representing FLM, board member Susan Robinson and I joined a team of BGF engineers and builders (Eplee, Jack Horn, Howard Pape, and others) who flew in to assess the situation on the ground.

As for me, it was a therapeutic experience — one I will never forget. I was relieved to be reunited with my 92-year-old father, who commented that the Bible warns of perilous times. Yet, he could not imagine anything more perilous than what he had witnessed with the earthquake. Half a million people, who had lost their homes, were living in tents in the most deplorable conditions.

BGF volunteer at work

Yet, in the midst of disaster, hope blossomed. Eplee, the BGF executive director, commented that "FLM Haiti is at the front end of great things." The earthquake changed everything, and out of tragedy came an opportunity to serve — broadening our scope of service in Haiti. On September 14, 2010, BGF and FLM agreed on a memorandum of understanding to respond to the reconstruction of Haiti. The two organizations agreed to engage in construction projects in Thomassin and Boutilliers, two communities served by FLM, during the period of September 2010 through December 2013. The work would include construction related to these FLM ministries:

a) Boutilliers Church

b) Thomassin volunteer residence

c) Thomassin replacement housing

d) Thomassin Trade School

BOUTILLIERS CHURCH

One of the most amazing developments in this reconstruction process was the commitment to rebuild the Boutilliers Church. Built by my grandfather, the church sits on the top of a high hill. After a winding road that traverses the steep cliffs and heights, one has to park the car in a small space and then climb 205 concrete-block steps to the church. The church, which has served as a community center for the mountainside village for decades, was destroyed by the earthquake while a Bible study was in session. Four people, including my cousin, Micheline, lost their lives. I led the BGF team to the ruins of the church as our first stop in a tour of the areas impacted by the quake. They were moved — but at that point, did not commit to rebuilding the church — wanting instead to focus more on aiding schools and hospitals, which they thought was more befitting of a humanitarian organization.

However, upon reporting to a donor all that BGF had seen at the church, and its usefulness in the life of the community, the donor allotted all funds necessary for its reconstruction. Eplee rightly underscores,

"The visit was a turning point for BGF outreach. Before that [visit], there was a hesitancy by its Board to invest resources in rebuilding faith community buildings. However, the visit to the Boutilliers community convinced BGF volunteers that a faith community and its building can be a vital center for community life, both for those of that particular faith and for area residents through its education and medical outreach programs."

The Boutilliers Church construction began in September of 2010 with a design by architect Roger Birle and engineer Brian Koerner. Jack Horn Jr. served as the volunteer project manager. He oversaw the on-site work of Taylor Quarles, the field manager, who lived in Thomassin while the structure was being built. The construction required hundreds of tons of concrete, sand, and steel to be carried by hand up more than 200 steps to the church site, which was accomplished only with the generous work of many members of the church and the local community. Forty-six BGF volunteers worked 3,350 hours, side by side with hundreds of local volunteers and workers.

Two years later, in January 2012, the church opened its doors in a special dedication service. The wife of the generous donor, who made it all possible, attended that service and recalls to this day, "That it was one of the most memorable moments, hearing the choir sing and feeling the Spirit in that place." The Boutilliers Church became a favorite place for BGF volunteers to visit when they came to Haiti. They especially liked to stop by and catch the choir practicing while watching the sun set over Port-au-Prince.

KAY D' ESPERANS (HOUSE OF HOPE)

As many more visiting medical teams came to assist at the House of David Medical Clinic, precious resources had to be spent on expensive hotel space to house our mission workers. To accommodate our helpers and better leverage our resources, the vision was born to build a volunteer residence, the guest-house Kay D' Esperans, on top of the existing medical clinic. It would be a way to save and generate more funding. It would also serve as a resource center for community groups. The same donor who contributed to the Boutilliers Church also gave the funds to execute this project.

Kay D' Esperans was designed by architect Antonio Martinez, with construction beginning in December 2010, and with the oversight of volunteer project manager Joe Simpson. Brad Lovelace moved to Haiti for the first months to serve as the field manager to begin the project. Field managers Ethan Tate and Curt Hoffman finished the interior and details.

The values and reasons why BGF and FLM built the guesthouse are so beautifully expressed on the FLM website: "The facility provides safe, comfortable, and affordable accommodations for mission teams during their stay in Haiti. It serves as a symbol of hope for the Haitian community as teams partner with the Haitian people; and it has become a community space of learning, sharing for business, health promotions, weddings, and other positive social enterprise." The new housing quarters can accommodate up to 22 volunteers at a time.

Shortly after the guesthouse opened, the University of Virginia's Darden School of Business became involved in designing a management plan for Kay D' Esperans. The university connected a few graduate students — those interested in a project on the developing world — in a partnership with FLM and BGF. It was an educational experience to allow the graduate students to immerse themselves in Haiti. The students developed a business plan for Kay D' Esperans that emphasized "safe, calm, and reliable accommodations for volunteers and visitors to Haiti." After living in Haiti and at the guesthouse, the students' plan stressed the importance of employing a house manager, and creating advertisements to reach neighborhood groups (along with local and foreign visitors) on how they could use the guesthouse. The recommendations enabled Kay D' Esperans to become a source of revenue for the ministry. The funds generated support the operation of the clinic and other projects.

BGF and FLM team evaluating the earthquake disaster in Haiti

It was a well-received plan, and visitors to the guesthouse often found their stays there to be magical. B. Denise Hawkins is a writer from Virginia. She traveled to Haiti (and in mission with FLM) several times. On each journey, she stayed at Kay D' Esperans. Before she went out into the streets of Haiti looking for stories, she always discovered that her "first stories resonated in the camaraderie and melody of the guesthouse. They are found in the voices of prayer-filled volunteers, and in the believers outside my bedroom window, singing softly their morning hymns in the church next door. And, as I stand on the patio, in the sweeping view of God's creation, my heart beats a joyous rhythm. The magic that is the guesthouse is a song of Haiti I'll carry with me always."

TI-KAY: HOUSING PROJECT FOR EARTHQUAKE VICTIMS

According to official estimates and various other news sources during those years, an estimated 250,000 homes were destroyed, displacing 1.3 million people. Tent villages sheltering tens of thousands of families were commonplace, and some even exist today. On one visit, a donor was so moved that they requested that BGF work with its partners to locate families who were in dire need of housing.

BGF began the Ti-Kay housing program in August 2011, with a house designed by architect Mike Stoneking. After studying dozens of traditional Haitian village homes, Stoneking drew a "ti-kay" — a little house that was panelized for mobility and designed according to international housing standards in rural areas. It was hurricane, termite, and earthquake resistant, while embracing traditional Haitian design.

Image of earthquake disaster in Port-au-Prince

Working in Haiti's coastal community of Leogane,

BGF built three homes per week, and then transported them to sites found in collaboration with FLM and l'Alliance d'Action Chrétienne. Distribution of the homes began in the Thomassin community, but then found more appropriate use in the devastated and rapidly growing suburbs of Port-au-Prince and in Croix-des-Bouquets, a community about 12 miles from the capital. According to Kelly Eplee, "With a contribution of $8 million, the partnership constructed about 1,000 homes in Haiti, re-homing an estimated 5,000 people, and employing 40 workers for five years. FLM was responsible for selecting families and aiding in logistics for around 400 of these homes."

EXCELSIOR TECHNICAL INSTITUTE

It has long been a dream of FLM Haiti to equip youth in the Thomassin area with marketable skills to enhance their job opportunities. This idea took root in the 1980s when talk began on the need to construct a multipurpose community center. MIPADEP ended up using that space as a K-13 school.

However, the idea never waned, and the urgency for reconstruction after the earthquake strongly revived and highlighted the need for skilled workers. As a nonprofit based in the construction trades, BGF took a particular interest in this project. To meet this need through FLM, the trade school was to be built on a parcel of land adjoining (and originally purchased for) the House of David Clinic. Steve Davis again stepped up as the volunteer architect and produced a design that eventually won awards. We're also thankful for the work of Clive Fox, the engineer who spent much time incorporating earthquake precautionary features.

The first prominent task was fundraising. According to Eplee, "It was fortunate that the Dave Matthews Band members claimed Charlottesville as home — and knew several BGF volunteers and their commitment to serve Haiti. They demonstrated interest through the BAMA Works Foundation, and invited me to Charlottesville to present the project at a social event."

It worked! They embraced the project. In June 2010, I was in Haiti when I received news of a breakthrough for the construction of a technical school in Thomassin. The Dave Matthews Band awarded a matching grant of $265,000 for the construction. It was a huge investment in the project. It was also a huge challenge for us to match the grant within a year. BGF steadfastly remained engaged in fundraising.

DESIGN CONCEPT: The Haiti Trade School Project

As for FLM, our campaign was coordinated by the remarkable Jim Strang. After college, Strang spent several years in biomedical research and co-authored three scientific publications. He then transitioned into health services administration where he spent the next 20+ years in various management capacities, including serving at the President/CEO level. Subsequently, he was a partner in a management consulting firm, and later executive director of a therapeutic equestrian center. He served as interim executive presbyter of two presbyteries of the Presbyterian Church USA. He assisted numerous nonprofit organizations as an advisor in the areas of management, financial development, and strategic planning.

Jim Strang

God sent him to us after the 2010 earthquake. He and his wife, Mary, went to Haiti as members of our first medical mission trip in the summer of 2000. After a while, he moved to Ohio and we practically lost contact. After the earthquake, he came and told me that he was willing and ready to help Haiti. He joined our board, and his commitment took FLM Haiti to a new level of excellence. It was amazing to watch Strang drive 111 miles, the driving distance from Akron, Ohio to Pittsburgh to attend board meetings every month for about a decade.

Strang also volunteered to lead the fight as chairman of the fundraising committee. As our treasurer and point man, he worked with BGF to coordinate the campaign. Just as the prophet Nehemiah engineered the reconstruction of the ruined walls of

Jerusalem, Strang designed the Nehemiah Project 2010 as a capital campaign to build the technical school. Building Goodness Foundation also conducted an effort to help come up with the funds. By June 2011 the partnership of FLM/BGF successfully raised the $265,000 necessary to meet the Dave Matthews matching request.

The groundbreaking ceremony for the Excelsior Technical Institute (ETI) took place on June 26, 2011. Work on the school started in November 2011, and, after amending the original design, the building would have two stories. Construction began in January 2012 and was completed in January 2013. The volunteer project manager was Joe Milby. Clay Clark, the field manager, lived in Thomassin for the duration of the project, which was completed in March 2013.

The dedication of ETI took place in the presence of board members Molly Golando, James Brown, and Jim Moran. A group of journalists from the Pittsburgh Black Media Federation, along with Maggie Hill of Boston, and a longtime friend and FLM supporter, Colleen Taylor of New York, were also in attendance. Taylor promised right then to get some 20 computers through Capital Bank for the school. Eplee, who attended the dedication, wrote the following comments: "At the dedication of this structure, there was an impressive gathering of FLM board members and Thomassin residents, the BGF volunteers, the workers, various other educators, and people from the Haitian construction industry. There was an inspiring resolve, expressed repeatedly, to educate and build Haiti back with the strength and beauty reflected in the excellent new technical school. The new school was appropriately named with one of Leon's favorite exclamations, 'Excelsior!' "

In 2015, ETI held the first mandatory ministry-facilitated, teacher-training session. At the beginning, 249 students signed up for the program. These were students from the community, and they attended ETI to receive instruction on computer basics and the use of the Internet. ETI also offered programs in electrical and plumbing training.

Birdy Reynolds, who worked at the University of Pittsburgh's Learning Research and Development Center, a place dedicated to documenting the impact on teaching and learning of curricular materials, made the decision to serve as a missionary in Haiti to assist with the opening of ETI. She departed for Haiti in October 2005 and became a trailblazing, long-term, on-site FLM missionary worker.

Despite political instability and violence, the Excelsior Technical Institute still serves. It remains one of the few professional schools and academies of higher education in the community of Thomassin and the surrounding areas. It continues to train professionals who meet the needs of the labor market. We do not work for profit, but rather for the social advancement of young people in the community.

MEDICAL MISSION CONTINUED

Our first post-earthquake medical mission took place in April 2010. Our team of 19 people, including four physicians, accomplished much in the week we spent there. Some screened more than 300 students at the school. Others provided care to some 500 patients. At a church in Kenscoff, a thin and frail 50-year-old woman was diagnosed with a collapsed lung. She had to be carried down the hill to a vehicle and be taken to the Baptist Mission Hospital. Our presence helped save many lives.

The earthquake disaster brought a new surge of interest for volunteerism. During the winter of 2011, three teams totaling 44 volunteers followed one another in service to Haiti. They all stayed at the newly built guesthouse, Kay D' Esperans, the House of Hope. These volunteers devoted themselves to touching the lives of Haitian families. Some provided medical care at the House of David Clinic, while others trained Haitians in the skills of giving first aid. In addition to the physical exams and dental fluoridation they were given, our students were also touched by the inspiring teaching they received in Bible study, the arts, and sciences.

FLM Haiti medical mission team

The medical mission grew even stronger with the addition of more teams. In October 2012, the Hebron Presbyterian Church of Pittsburgh sent a mission team to Haiti in partnership with FLM. Twelve to 15 people went, including Mary Gregg and board member Jim Moran. Some team members did plumbing work in churches in the community. Others under the leadership of Isabel Smith, the Hebron mission team leader, attended to issues related to women's health and hygiene. Their presentations and the products were very well received. They spoke about female bodies, how to care for them and keep them healthy, and how to avoid infections. Smith commented, "Can't say how moved we all were to be able to participate in this ministry. I felt like we really connected with the women. They hugged us and thanked us, and we were definitely blessed to be a blessing."

Reverend David Robinson, who gave Leon the idea for a medical clinic, passed away in 2004 before the medical clinic was built. House of David Community Medical Clinic is named after him.

In December 2014, Cathy Sapp led a mission team to Haiti with a focus on feeding the hungry. She is a child development specialist who became the first Black woman to serve as deputy mayor of the Penn Hills Council. (In December 2021, she was elected mayor.)

Sapp's team passed out some 700 bags of dry food at our school and to employees at our clinic. Her team also held activities with the preschoolers. Her sister, Anica Jones, provided funds for many years for the canteen, a special initiative used to purchase food for school students. Sapp's team returned to Haiti in December 2015, and distributed food again at the school and the church next to our campus.

We were also blessed to have a team from Rodef Shalom of Pittsburgh under the dynamic leadership of Marian Allen. She played a major role in our interfaith mission of education and health. She saw her experience as "a call to heal." Describing and reflecting on her service in Haiti, she wrote, "I explored several nonprofit agencies doing mission work in Haiti. I discovered Functional Literacy Ministry (FLM) of Haiti, a Pittsburgh-based Christian group. Although I am Jewish, I believe that sharing purpose and goodness has no religious boundaries. So, I took the leap and traveled with FLM to Haiti for the first time in 2011. My role was to help provide basic health care and education. It was a profound and life-changing experience. I made a second Mission with FLM in 2012.

"After each trip, I returned to my own spiritual home, Rodef Shalom Congregation, in Pittsburgh, and shared my experiences in the context of the Jewish obligation of Tikkun Olam, which can be translatcd as Repair the World. As Jews, we are taught that we each have a responsibility to partner with God to help repair and heal the world. As others heard about my time in Haiti, the idea of organizing a congregational service trip formed. I approached the Rev. Pamphile with the idea of a Jewish trip to Haiti, and he was wonderfully supportive. Rodef Shalom Congregation was the first Jewish group to arrange a trip through FLM.

Marian Allen, head of Rodef Shalom mission team

"The planning began for a 2013 trip to Haiti. We assembled 13 Pittsburghers from within our congregation and the community-at-large, including our Rabbi Sharyn Henry. Among us were medical professionals, an electrician, artists, teachers, translators, a printmaker, and two young people, all committed to helping at FLM's school and medical clinic. Our activities were wide-reaching, from providing health care to teaching English and initiating art projects at the school, to conducting vision tests at the clinic and distributing eyeglasses that we'd collected from the Pittsburgh community, to rewiring FLM's guesthouse. We even taught Haitian children a beloved Jewish hymn, *Hinei Ma Tov*, which translates, "How good it is to be together."

Duffle bags of medicines for medical missions

"Rabbi Henry also found the trip very enriching. She brought an inspiring sermon to our church in Thomassin. It certainly showed God's miraculous work in bringing Haitians and Americans together. Rabbi Henry said, 'The Haitians have taught us so much that it will be weeks and months before we will fully understand all of the lessons you have taught us. This week, you and I have looked at one another as we have labored beside each other to heal and to teach. We have seen the divine spark in one another; we have seen each other's humanity—our strengths, our challenges, our joys, our sorrows. And we have come to understand that we are brothers and sisters.'"

FLM's response to the earthquake was significant and productive. In collaboration with BGF, a robust effort was made in providing relief and a strong engagement in the reconstruction of some affected areas of the country. The FLM/BGF partnership was a powerful manifestation of the noble principle that TOGETHER WE ACHIEVE THE EXTRAORDINARY.

CHAPTER 6
LOVE ALWAYS EQUIPS:
EDUCATION MISSION

The year 2004 marked the bicentennial independence of Haiti. Yet counter to this very context, Haiti was again ensnared in the midst of chaos. *The Los Angeles Times* reported, "The Bicentennial Tower was supposed to be the centerpiece of celebrations marking the 200th anniversary of Haiti's independence, in a year intended to inspire a new direction for the world's first Black republic after a long history of abject poverty and autocratic rule. But from the gunfire-pocked January 1 ceremonies to the violence still consuming the capital's slums, 2004 has served only to showcase Haitians' pain and failures."

President Jean-Bertrand Aristide, who was re-elected a second time as president, was again widely contested by the opposition parties. Armed conflict broke out in Gonaïves. The fighting spread out to other cities. Gradually, insurgents took control of Northern Haiti. Aristide was forced out of office for a second time. Haiti once again became unstable and insecure.

VACATION BIBLE SCHOOL

This instability affected the FLM mission team's travel plans. Our summer medical mission trip did not take place as usual. Only five people, including Mary Gregg, Maggie Hill, Sue Robinson, Donnie Hanning, and I made the journey that year. In the absence of healthcare service, our team had to monitor and adjust. We then turned our attention to the 377 students at MIPADEP and the 150 students at the Boutilliers Church. Inspired by the Vacation Bible School (VBS) model, we opted to minister to these students through a program consisting of Bible stories, music, games, and English lessons. This new format worked and became the first step toward developing the new dimension of education mission. In light of this experience, Mary Gregg, at the November 2004 board meeting, shared the idea to continue this educational dimension for our mission trips. To make this idea a reality, it became necessary to have a coordinator.

The Vacation Bible School model made headway with our longtime board member, Carol Williams. She eagerly devoted herself to the project and divided the mission week into two segments. She focused Monday and Tuesday on younger children, while the rest of the week was focused on teenagers. She made it a time of Bible learning, devotions, and fellowship. The education mission team of 2006 held a camp for 600 children. With the help of Susan Robinson, representatives of 14 churches in Hamburg, New York met to pack supplies for the education team.

Students were thrilled to learn about science, stories of creation, and the sculpting of art. Dudley Hollenbeck, who taught in inner-city high schools for 35 years in the Buffalo, New York, area, was a specialist in motivating unmotivated students. He confessed, however, "I did not need that skill in Haiti; the Thomassin students were all eager to learn." Hollenbeck also described the after-school program, which offered additional lessons in science, music, art, and games. He noted, "Many students stayed for these courses, and I worked each day with about 30 students who wanted to learn more about space travel. Most of them had no knowledge that man had been to the moon or there were other planets." Beside Hollenbeck, Dave Shankland, a sculptor, artist, teacher, and humanitarian activist from Ohio, taught sculpture. His students carved and painted birds and turtles, which they took home at the end of the week.

Board member Carol Williams served faithfully

Vacation Bible School was meaningful for both Haitian students and their American teachers. One education team member commented, "I saw plenty of trials for the people of Haiti, but I also saw hope and progress. Our Bible story was the story of the paralytic whose friends lowered him by ropes through a roof so that Jesus could heal him. Our team feels so honored to have 'held hopes' for our Haitian friends these weeks. As we looked through that opening, we so clearly saw Jesus."

Linda Ross Brown, a former music teacher in the Pittsburgh Public schools, was a member of the education team. She started a choir and rhythm group, and her class was the largest, even though the students had to walk a distance from school to church. For a week, she taught music at MIPADEP. She conducted a choir of 140 rich voices that could be heard down the road and across the cornfield. She found the students "joyful and enthusiastic as they sang with their whole body, mind, and soul. Young and seasoned voices alike sang wholeheartedly in church services." At week's end, ensembles large and small, plus soloists, poured all of their talent and creativity into a program of soul-stirring songs for family and friends. Ross Brown shared this realization: "The presence of God, FLM's impact, and music in their lives helped me understand how the Haitians can live with hope while in abject poverty."

EDUCATION MISSION TEAMS

The focus on education became a reality by gaining further ground and greater interest. A much-needed coordinator emerged when the Rev. Molly Golando, from Hamburg, New York, joined FLM Haiti in 2009. She brought a new level of excellence to our education mission. (Golando has bachelor's and master's degrees in music teacher education. She also has training in theological and ministerial studies, and is serving as a pastor in Western New York.) When she came on board in 2009, she had activities for both students and teachers. The primary students attended a Vacation Bible School format with the theme of "Healthy Bodies, Minds and Souls." The theme verse of the week was Psalm 139:14 (NKJV): "I will praise You, for I am fearfully and wonderfully made; marvelous are Your works; and that my soul knows very well." All of the children learned the song: "I'm Inright, Outright, Upright, Downright Happy All The Time." They learned skills for journaling, played games, completed coloring pages, listened to stories of their heritage and connection to the proud people of Africa, and heard the story of the paralytic from Mark 2.

Tyra Good, Education Mission Team member

TEACHER SEMINARS

A higher level was attained still when the idea surfaced that FLM should add teacher seminars and training to its education work. In reality, it was a strategy that came into being in 1986, when Rev. Jack Kennedy of Christian Literacy Associates of Pittsburgh held a seminar for our literacy teachers and other interested individuals. It was an opportunity to train the teachers in using the Creole primers, bought with funds donated to FLM by the Bible Distribution Center in Pittsburgh.

It was Rev. Golando who first turned her attention to the teachers at our MIPADEP school. She discovered that they desired to have materials and training. Thereupon she implemented the teaching of new strategies and incorporated relevant changes in the curriculum. She achieved this goal by starting to hold seminars for the teachers. She was ably assisted in her first summer of 2011 by Dr. Edward Davis of the St. Albans Presbyterian Church in New York and Baptist minister Dr. Paul Hicks.

The teacher professional development seminar of 2011 was attended by 36 teachers. They came from our school, the surrounding area and some from as far as Port-au-Prince. The success of the seminar could be measured through the teachers' consistent attendance throughout the week and their positive feedback.

The program continued in 2012, involving 10 team members and a total of 50 participants from six neighboring schools. That seminar covered a wide range of topics, such as brain research discoveries, learning styles, time management, creative techniques for science curriculum, and so forth. Birdy Reynolds, who was one of the instructors at that seminar, relayed, "Our time with the teachers and administrators was productive; they worked hard and accomplished so much! Unlike in the U.S., where prayer is banned in schools, we had the liberty to pray before our sessions, and they expected it! One of the lessons I prepared was on genetic inheritance. Through our discussions, I had the opportunity to share how science and spirituality are not in conflict. We are made in God's image and we have the mind of Christ. He gives us wisdom to know the mysteries of the Kingdom, to solve problems, and to be agents of change."

EXPANDING THE TEACHER SEMINARS

The teacher seminars were greatly enriched with the involvement of Dr. Rhonda Taliaferro of Pittsburgh. Taliaferro is a seasoned educator. For more than 35 years, she was a teacher and administrator with the Pittsburgh Public Schools. She served as principal at the Creative and Performing Arts (CAPA) Middle School. Though retired, she continues to serve in education as a part-time university supervisor in the Education Department at Chatham University in Pittsburgh. In gratitude, she serves with FLM Haiti's educational colleagues to empower children in Haiti.

Dr. Rhonda Taliaferro

Taliaferro was active in the Teacher Training, Summer 2015 — *Tout Moun Ka Aprann!* (Everyone Can Learn). Here is how she described the event: "The fall, winter, and spring planning (through telephone conferencing with the education team and members from Boston, Western New York, and California) was interesting and purposeful. Here, I could use my skills and talents as an educational instructional leader to help shape the five-day professional development experience for the anticipated 100 K-6 Haitian teachers who came from miles around Thomassin, and who looked forward to professional growth from the week-long summer training. Our learning goal, based on what Bishop Pamphile had mentioned to us, was to provide Haitian teachers needed strategies to address classroom management to support academic achievement. To that end, the education team decided to focus on classroom management and learning styles framed by Howard Gardner's Theory of Multiple Intelligence (MI), where every person learns best matched to one or several of the eight (8) multiple intelligences in learning.

"Teachers took the MI assessment and were surprised to know their intelligence style and its effect on teaching and learning. Similarly, we wanted teachers to know their strengths in MI and how to teach to their students' MI. We learned that most Haitian teachers teach students, all 40+ students in the same classroom, using a direct instruction method. We found that by showing our Haitian colleagues how to use the MI theory in teaching that teachers could use a variety of ways to engage those 40+ students using one or more of the eight intelligences: linguistic, mathematical/logical, spatial, kinesthetic/movement, musical, interpersonal, intrapersonal, and naturalistic, based on the needs of the student. Students can learn based on their learning style. *Tout moun ka aprann!* (Everyone can learn).

Teachers attending FLM seminar

"Our American mission team learned that our

Haitian colleagues responded positively to a different approach to teaching and learning during the summer institute in 2015. We arranged a follow-up visit to Haiti with our teaching colleagues in January 2016 to observe how they were doing, and to let each colleague visit one another to observe and give feedback on what they observed. Teachers noted their satisfaction with learning about Multiple Intelligence and learning styles, and how they would apply such in their classrooms. Thursday and Friday of the training week was dedicated to planning with their principals on how they would use MI in their classroom instruction and relate it to their content areas — and deciding what support, if any, the teachers would need."

Birdy Reynolds, who was also involved in that summer teacher institute, described her experience as exhilarating. She said, "I collaborated with other teacher educators. We focused on learning styles and continued our work on restorative justice, which was led by a team member from California. Again, the daylong sessions were so productive. We had 120 teacher participants, including teachers from our school, MIPADEP, and others from surrounding schools. It was incredible to know that many of the teachers walked for hours to attend the sessions. I recall one gentleman who wore the same powder blue two-piece suit every day; but each day it was clean, and he took such pride in engaging in the discussions."

TEACHER SEMINARS 2016-2017

Teacher training seminars continued to grow in popularity in the Thomassin community and beyond. Taliaferro again reported on the 2016 and 2017 sessions, both implemented and united under the theme, "Engage!"

"As we prepared to engage in summer teacher trainings, I held the 2017 summer packing day for the education team from Pittsburgh at my house, a week before our departure. All packing bags were spread out on my front lawn and in my living room area. About a dozen FLM supporters brought in school supplies in bulk, as well as vitamins and other things to pack. Each traveling team member agreed to pay an additional $35 for an extra bag of education supplies to go on JetBlue to Haiti. Following the two-hour labor-intensive bag-filling and weighing, I served dinner on my back patio where all could rest and enjoy each other in our pre-journey interaction.

"Fortunately, I got my travel inoculation shots from the Allegheny County Health Department two weeks prior, had little reaction, and enough energy to get us moving with bag packing!"

Rev. Molly Golando, chair of the FLM Education Mission Team

In addition to Taliaferro, the 2016 and 2017 teacher training teams included the chair of the FLM Education Mission Team, Molly Golando, a retired teacher from western New York, and several of her retired teacher friends from the same area. It also included Maggie Hill, a retired teacher from Boston, retired teacher Susan Robinson, and Birdy Reynolds from Pittsburgh. Participating also was a team from Los Angeles, led by attorney Rosalyn Lee, and composed of current educators, a school social worker, and education advocates. The team planned to train on restorative justice, which spoke to ways of mediation and proactive community building in the classroom, instead of punitive discipline as a way of dealing with classroom management. Taliaferro recalled, "Restorative justice was a hit!!"

FLM Instructors leading a teacher seminar

The teacher training theme, Engage, was designed to build on the lessons gained from the two prior summers, focusing on Multiple Intelligence and learning styles. Taliaferro says that the teams were laser-focused with Engage — in order to make a difference in how Haitian teachers learn to increase student engagement and decrease classroom management issues. Based on teacher practice sessions, collaborative observation, and surveys with the teachers, the Haitian educators overwhelmingly felt they had strengthened:

- their classroom management and student engagement skills;
- their mastery of how and when to praise and congratulate students for making efforts;
- their ability to teach students to work in groups.

"It was also wonderful," recalled Taliaferro, "to see principals in the same classrooms learning with teachers and building a climate of trust and learning together." In the context of seminars, team members worked not only with teachers but also with administrators, who benefited as well from the opportunity to sharpen their skills. Mission accomplished in the 2016 and 2017 ENGAGE!!

Besides working in the classroom, team members sought to support the school financially. In 2011, Susan Robinson established a sponsorship program designed to help fund teachers' salaries, provide daily lunches to students, and purchase textbooks and other classroom materials.

In addition, team members were also concerned with the health of students and teachers. To address the issue of clean water, which affected them all, FLM partnered with the organization Water for Life to provide clean water in Haiti. Elena Delgado was the representative of this organization. During the education mission of January 2016, she distributed 120 filters in Thomassin, Kenscoff, and Fort Jacques. In subsequent years, physicians also dedicated special attention to the school, providing physicals for all of our 600 students.

Our education mission teams make a difference in improving education in the Thomassin community and beyond. Their efforts have touched the lives of students, teachers, and principals. The importance and meaning of their work remain a durable investment in the different communities where we have been privileged to serve.

CHAPTER 7
LOVE ALWAYS PROMOTES UNDERSTANDING: CULTURAL MISSIONS

By Ervin Dyer

A few friends — a group of U.S. journalists, photographers, and I — board the back of *God is Love* (the name drawn on the colorful *Tap-Tap*, one of the privately owned taxis in Port-au-Prince, the capital of Haiti). It is not yet noon as we head for the airport, after spending a week exploring the cultural mosaic that is part of this sun-bright island nation. We have danced in dimly-lit, pulsating nightclubs. We have eaten red beans and rice in the stately suburb of Petionville. And we have traipsed up the mountain to the glorious Citadelle Laferrière, a worn-but-majestic fortress built in the north of the nation in the early 1800s by newly independent Haitians as a sentinel against further French invasion.

As we ride along, we share memories and laughs of our adventures in this grand nation. As we approach the heavy traffic and the snail's pace of navigating through congested Port-au-Prince, the tap-tap practically slows to a crawl.

A young girl — she looks to be about 9 or 10 years old — approaches the tap-tap. She is saying something, but she is speaking in a language we don't understand. Is it German? We continue to crawl through traffic. She continues to follow. She continues to speak. Is it Italian? She makes her way through several other languages. We recognize the Spanish, but none of us is fluent enough to translate. Finally, she makes her way to English: "Please, help me," she says, holding out her hands. We realize the little girl does not know who we are or where we are from. Yet somehow, at her young age, she has learned to speak several foreign languages. To do so increases her odds of connecting with a larger portion of visitors to Haiti, who might be able to hand her the alms that she might use to feed herself or her family.

The little girl, with her tattered clothing and urgent pleas, is a reminder of the poverty and inequality that chokes Haiti. But her grasp of languages — and that she accesses so many at such a tender age, (especially in a nation where large chunks of young people don't have any access to a formal education) — is a reminder of Haiti's hope.

We see the face of God in this child. We see a humanity that deserves love, justice, relief, and possibility. She is deserving of God's love, so she is deserving of ours. We reach in our pockets and hand her what we can ... and she accepts and runs away.

Street scene in downtown Cap-Haitien, northern Haiti /photo by Germaine Watkins

PARTNERING WITH FLM
IN CULTURAL MISSIONS

The image of the little girl lives with me. Her story reminds me of why — before Haiti's current political and social unrest (when it was much safer to travel into Haiti) — I took storytellers, such as writers, photographers, sociologists, and other creative professionals, to the land of green mountains ... And we began to write about Haiti, host podcasts, post our images on social media, and hold community forums once we arrived back in America. It was all work that we did in partnership with the Functional Literacy Ministry of Haiti, or FLM Haiti. We wanted to share stories on the fullness of Haiti, a fullness that is so often not a part of its narrative. We were called to Haiti to cultivate a different message: Yes, Haiti has poverty, but it also has potential.

I became more intimately aware of Haiti about two decades ago. Leon Pamphile, a Haiti native, worked as a teacher and preacher in Pittsburgh. At the time, he called the local newspaper where I worked and asked if we could put in a brief notice about local celebrations recognizing Haiti's anniversary of independence from France.

I was considered to be the paper's chief reporter on African and Black culture matters, and Pamphile's call was directed to me. The more I chatted with Pamphile, now a bishop serving some of the most impoverished communities in Haiti, the more I became interested in how he climbed from rural Haiti to become a U.S. citizen and earn a Ph.D from the University of Pittsburgh.

By the end of our conversation, I had encouraged Pamphile to let me write a feature on his life. We became friends. Eventually, Pamphile invited me to Haiti, to see the work he was doing to bring literacy, medical care, and hope to the people in the valleys and hills where he walked as a child. Led by his Christian

**Street scene in old Jacmel, a coastal community in Haiti
/photo by Ervin Dyer**

**In front of the presidential palace, 2005, in Port-au-Prince. The
palace was destroyed in the 2010 earthquake. /photo by Ervin Dyer**

faith, he founded FLM Haiti to give back to the people of his homeland. It was an incredible mission. But I was neither a doctor, a dentist, nor formally trained as a teacher. What role could I fill to make a more significant contribution to FLM than being someone who carried a duffle bag full of medicines up the mountain? While this task is important, I felt called to offer a greater purpose. *How could I call on my talents and skills as a journalist and professional communicator to make a more positive contribution?* Soon, I created what I called "cultural missions," taking journeys into Haiti to get to know its arts, food, faith, history, and people. Working in tandem with FLM, we stayed at the nonprofit's guesthouse, we used FLM translators, and we enlisted friends of FLM to be our tour guides. Of course, this kind of partnership supported FLM, because it raised funds and bolstered the community of Haitians dependent on FLM to help them earn a living.

CASTING HAITI IN A NEW LIGHT

And the cultural missions did something more. It allowed the visitors who came with me to march deeper into Haiti's humanity — its proud history, arts, culture, spirit, and geographic splendors. Not only did we get to the mountaintop of the Citadelle, but we also walked the white-sand shores of Jacmel. We toured the National Museum of History and saw relics from the conquest when Columbus came — and we discovered more about the Taino, the indigenous people of the island, who were there before the first enslaved Africans were forcibly shipped over.

We also became friends with our Haitian guides. We saw the work they were doing in the community to bring clean water, housing, education, and hope to their families and neighbors. In many ways, their efforts were a mirror of the work of FLM. With two of the gentlemen, Jimmy Pierre and Wadson Desir, we created a small travel enterprise. We used Pierre and Desir to scout safe locations and provide information on how we might travel there, and where we might stay when visiting. We "hired" them to be our translators and guides on our cultural tours.

Sam Bojarski was a recent graduate of the University of Pittsburgh and an emerging professional journalist when he traveled to Haiti on one of the cultural missions. He came along because he was intrigued after hearing me talk so much about the nation. He was also a curious young man who was interested in how economic development had played out in the post-colonial world. Sam wanted to learn and see for himself some of the stark imbalances between the global north and global south.

Bojarski had this to say about his visit to Haiti: "I think the idea of the trip captivated me because it clashed with the picture of Haiti I had in my head. Because the only real image I had was the bad side. I vividly remember watching news reports of the 2010 earthquake, and a little later in life I would educate myself on the country's turbulent political history. But with the cultural mission, I couldn't ever imagine getting a more complete 'taste' of the real Haiti in less than a week. We saw the work of brilliant artists in Jacmel and experienced what is still the most awe-inspiring place I've ever been — the Citadelle in the far north. Of course, I also got a close-up sense of how unequal the society is, winding down roads flanked by high concrete walls erected by wealthy homeowners, while underemployed youth in Port-au-Prince sold food and small goods to make ends meet."

At the end of his journey, Bojarski began freelancing with the *Haitian Times* newspaper for almost two years, and for a while, worked there full time. He was also part of a team that was awarded a Pulitzer Center grant to report on how Haiti has fared 10 years

**American college students interacting with
Haitian students /photo by Ervin Dyer**

after the earthquake — and was able to share insights
from his Pulitzer stories at a University of Pittsburgh
community forum.

It was a similar experience for Pittsburgh pho-
tographer Germaine Watkins. He made his first visit
to Haiti in 2017, and remembers that it forever altered
his view of how he saw the country. Here's what he
said:

> "For years I've heard about missionary trips
> to Haiti — how they are life-changing and re-
> freshing for the soul. But what the mainstream
> media showed me about Haiti was something
> that didn't appeal to me. When I became in-
> volved with a black photographers group, we
> were introduced to journalist Erv Dyer. After
> talking with Dr. Dyer about his trips to Haiti,
> he encouraged me to consider traveling there.
> My first trip there was to show Haiti through
> the eyes of a photographer, capturing the side
> that is less reported."

Once in Haiti, Watkins recalled how his eyes were opened. He likened his experience to an iceberg, where what you first see is only the tip — an outer portion that only highlights the most obvious elements of blight. "But," he also said, "Once you're immersed in the experience of Haiti, you see the beauty, resilience, pride, and potential. The image that comes to mind every time I think of Haiti is that of a young girl in a sparkling white dress holding the hand of someone — very likely her mother — who is also in a sparkling white dress among the dust and debris in the streets."

Watkins realizes there is so much that is needed to lift up Haiti; but when he returned to Pittsburgh from his travels there, he helped to organize a photography exhibition, "Haiti: Behind the Headlines." He said: "I did this to showcase Haiti in a positive light and to bring recognition that more was happening in Haiti besides poverty. This exhibition helped to inspire others to donate to Haiti and consider participating in missionary and cultural missions trips."

Watkins traveled to Haiti again the following year. When he returned, he shared his experiences during a radio broadcast, community lecture, and two other photographic exhibitions. When Bojarski and Watkins went back into the community to share their thoughts on Haiti, their sharing highlighted what we felt was an important component to the cultural tours. After the tours were finished, we wanted participants to head back into their home communities in the United States to begin sharing all they had seen, heard, and learned.

And they did. Our cultural mission participants wrote newspaper articles on their travels. They developed radio podcasts. They designed photography exhibitions. And just like Bojarski and Watkins had done, they held public forums — teaching, explaining, and answering questions on the complexity and beauty that they had experienced in Haiti.

Why was this important?

Each engagement and media production offered us the opportunity to cast Haitians in a new light, to characterize them in fuller, more human dimensions. To move them beyond the flat, dispiriting descriptor of "poorest nation in the Western Hemisphere." We wanted to show their culture and vast — though complicated — history (one that I always argue changed the world), and show them as people of flesh-and-blood-and-spirit.

As a Black American, though I'm a foreigner, an outsider when I travel to Haiti, much about being there has a familiarity. Haiti, for me, is like its smaller cousins, the urban Black communities of New York's Harlem, which I consider my spiritual home, or the African American neighborhoods of the Hill District and Homewood in Pittsburgh, the city where I live. Like any predominantly Black space, Haiti (and each of these places) has long suffered from the gaze of those who look at these communities and see nothing — except the resources that can be exploited and extrapolated: people, culture, and art.

Too many see these Black spaces only through the lens of biased media. For centuries, ill-formed narratives have blighted the humanity of Haitians and constructed the Caribbean nation as only a destitute place that offers nothing but disease, death, and deprivation.

My friend and Haitian scholar, Yven Destin, has studied how media images and coverage shape such a bleak and blighted frame about Haiti. In his work, he discovered that mainstream media often focused on Haitians as being needy boat people, HIV carriers, and uncivilized (a steady media distortion that left Haitians framed as threatening, polluted, and primitive).

Destin, like Bishop Pamphile, has roots in Haiti. His family immigrated from there before settling in Florida where he was born. He, like myself, understands that Haiti's song calls us to her — to explore her history, her culture and art, her meaning to the world. I met Destin in 2014, when we were both in graduate school at the University of Pittsburgh.

Resting at a Jacmel beach /photo by Kenneth Neely

OUR COMMON HERITAGE WITH HAITI

But years before Destin and I came to discuss and study Haiti, the siren of the lush land, once known as the Pearl of the Antilles, called to me from another writerly source: Langston Hughes. The Black American poet has had a deep influence on my life and writing career. Hughes visited Haiti in 1932 and befriended the Haitian writer and ethnographer Jacques Roumain. The two wrote about race, class, and oppression among the people of the African diaspora.

Hughes, in Haiti, discovered the joy of spending time with what he called "the people without shoes" — the hard-working everyday folks whose culture and lifestyle he embraced. I wanted to discover these people and find this joy, too. I wanted to walk where Hughes walked, and be inspired and renewed by taking the same journey. Following in the poet's foot-steps is part of what inspired my first visits to Haiti and, later, the cultural missions.

Like people who only know of Black spaces in the narrowest of ways, I, too, first feared Haiti. It was largely unknown to me. Most of what I'd read in U.S. newspapers concerned the home-grown terrorism of the Tonton Macoutes, a sort of marauding bogeyman force formed in 1959 to exert political control in Haiti. I knew little of the country's long history of oppression by Western powers, and little of its heroic turn from slavery to rebellion and freedom, to a downturn exacerbated by United States military occupation and a debilitating cycle of political coups and conflicts. And then, of course, the 2010 earthquake, and now, in recent years, the drama of kidnapping, violence, and political freefall.

So, when I first ventured over in 2008, my family prayed for me as I boarded the plane for Port-au-Prince. But after visiting Haiti for a week, I felt at home. There was something familiar about it. Visiting the rural areas was like visiting my grandmother's farm in Hanover County, Virginia.

Most intimately, what I saw was a people and a culture that reminded me of my grandmother and her way of life. I recognized the grace and fervor with which Haitians sang their worship hymns. I recognized the rice and chicken that was served for dinner. I recognized the way that, amid such insecurity, family and neighbors bonded to care for each other.

I learned that Haiti, despite its complicated challenges, can and should be defined by the rich and vibrant culture of its people and not the dark, one-dimensional media depictions. But more broadly, Haiti reminded me of me and where I came from. What I saw in Haiti was the same spirit I see in many Black spaces: a determination of its people to survive and live free. I saw their beautiful art, heard their beautiful music, and heard their pleas to work in partnership with others to make their nation better. In this Black space, I found my mission:

It is to share the story of Haiti, and other Black spaces, as fully as possible. We have to remember, despite its current troubles, Haiti is the land of magnificent heroes: Toussaint L'ouverture, the Haitian independence leader who chased away the enslaving French, is one of them. We have to remember it is a space where Haitian children are writing their own stories — in French and in Haiti Creole — a lyrical language worthy of survival and acknowledgment.

It is my prayer that political and spiritual goodwill will intervene and calm the tumult that ruptures Haiti. I long to return again one day to the museums that tell Haiti's history, to scale the heights of the imposing Citadelle fortress, and to be in song with the locals, hearing in their voices what they think of their nation's politics, culture, and challenges. With luck, we'll have these conversations over rice and beans, reminiscent of the meals and spirit shared at my grandmother's house.

History, culture, faith, food, and hope. Yes, Black spaces matter.The legacies of racism, stark and persistent inequality, and political malfeasance have played a role in delivering Haiti to a horrible present. Yet, in the midst of such lack, we must remember Haiti is a *human* place. We have to remember that being impoverished does not mean being without agency, power, or potential. The little girl we met on the way to the airport was empowered with a wealth of languages. That she possessed such skills is a reminder of the promise that is hidden in Haiti. That her condition of poverty forced her to use her skills to plead for food for her family, and not in preparation for a scholarship or further advancement, is the shame of Haiti — and indeed the world, as it looks on and does nothing to eliminate her obstacles.

Our goal, in how we communicate about Haitians and, indeed, the foundation of the work of FLM, is to help her uncover more of that promise.

That is why, one day, we must return to this island in the sun.

CHAPTER 8
LOVE ALWAYS HOPES

In the description of love in 1 Corinthians 13, we find four things love "always" does. Love is not just an idea; love is action. The third action listed is that love "always hopes." Love, seen in terms of relationships with others, promotes hope. It is a safeguard guaranteeing that we treat others right. Johann Goethe, the German thinker made this suggestion: "If we treat people as they ought to be, we help them become what they are capable of becoming." In a society like Haiti, where people are not treated as they ought to be treated, where they are left to themselves without basic public service and assistance, an organization such as FLM Haiti matters. We provide help with the conviction that, unlike their government, love will not give up on them. Love always hopes in order to bring God's purpose to pass. This chapter focuses on FLM Haiti's efforts to keep hope alive for God's people.

NURTURING HOPE THROUGH PRAYER

Prayer is the mighty weapon at the disposal of God's people. Recognizing our limitations as human beings, we welcome the privilege of prayer to advance our plan in the fight against poverty. Jesus set the right example for us. He had compassion for a large crowd that followed Him. As they were in a remote place, the disciples acknowledged their limitations and recommended sending the crowds away, so they could go to the villages and buy themselves some food. Jesus saw it otherwise. He took the available five loaves and the two fish and prayed: "Looking up to heaven, he gave thanks and broke the loaves. Then he gave them to the disciples. The disciples gave them to the people. They all ate and were satisfied" (Matthew 14:19-20).

When funds were lacking for the ministry, we readily used the weapon of prayer. It happened once in the early days of the ministry when we could not meet our regular monthly grant for Haiti. My wife, Rozelle, whose service to the FLM ministry is invaluable in many ways, turned to the Lord in prayer. She went to an all-night Friday prayer meeting at the Morningside Church of God in Christ in the Garfield neighborhood of the city. There she implored God's favor for provisions for the ministry. On Saturday morning, the very next day, the Lord sent two good-will donors with the needed funds: Our longtime supporter and colleague Barbara Kunschner showed up, and so did Rev. Dr. Ronald Glenn, a pastor and writer, and someone who became a longtime friend to FLM. They came in person to our doors to deliver their donations.

In another heart-warming example, board member Jim Moran, a fervent and faithful pastor on our mission teams, also used the weapon of prayer to comfort the sick. His wife Lynn recalls seeing him in action during our visits to Haiti: "Several times throughout the day, Jim (often serving as our spiritual leader on the trip) would be called to pray for a man or woman identified by one of our physicians or nurses as someone who needed prayer. These prayer requests varied — from our pastor having just learned from one of our doctors that the illness they have is serious; or for a person who has lost a spouse, child, or parent; to the devastating earthquake that tore Haiti apart on January 12, 2010, flattening homes and leaving children as orphans. (The reality of this terrible event continues to live with many Haitians every day.)

Jim could often be heard saying, "I will pray for the job for which you ask, but I hope this can help a little to ease your burden." Reaching into his pocket, he would provide money to share as he began to pray — reminding the parent that God is good and they should continue to pray without ceasing for their heartfelt family need. Their time together always ended with a huge hug to encourage them. It was Jim's way of showing his love for them, and demonstrating God's love for their family as well."

Rev. Dr. Jim Moran, FLM board member; Lynn Moran, FLM board member who organized the pharmacy in Haiti

Adrienne Kuhlengel, now practicing in Columbia, Pennsylvania, was a third-year medical student when she traveled to Haiti as part of our medical mission in 2009. Her encounter with some patients at the clinic highlighted the need to always hold on to hope. Adrienne shared, "I saw many people with classic symptoms of severe depression, and I fervently wished I had something to prescribe for them. With a resigned smile, they would talk about their sadness, about the people they have lost, about their inability to sleep, poor appetite, difficulty concentrating, poor energy, and their feelings of guilt about providing for their families." She confessed that she could only offer prayer, but counted it a privilege to pray with such people, who love God and depend on Him daily.

In 2005, Pastor Barry Sweet of the Crossroads Presbyterian Church in Washington, Pennsylvania, brought what he called "a new piece to the puzzle — namely evangelism and prayer. I had the honor, privilege, and joy to be allowed to pray with each person who came to our medical mission and to share the Gospel of Jesus Christ with them. I prayed for healing from disease, for food and water, for jobs, for freedom from persecution, and for freedom from the escalating violence and terrorism that has gripped Haiti in recent months."

FOSTERING HOPE WITH TRIUMPH BAPTIST CHURCH

Dr. Rhonda Moore Johnson serves as mission coordinator at Triumph Baptist Church in Pittsburgh. She is a Pittsburgh native, physician, and career health executive. Johnson has dedicated her professional life to improving the health of under-resourced and medically vulnerable populations in the United States and around the world. She practiced pediatrics and adolescent medicine in Albany, Georgia, and Cincinnati, Ohio. Johnson led the Triumph Church International Missions Team that served in Haiti for one week in 2016, 2017, and 2018. The team was composed of members of Triumph Church and other congregations. Team members traveled to Haiti from several states: Pennsylvania, New York, Texas, Arizona, Nevada, Washington, and Georgia.

Their vision is transporting the love of Christ into all of the world, and proclaiming the gospel to the whole creation. Their mission is a commitment to provide help, hope, and healing to the impoverished, broken, and sick by advancing the Kingdom of God abroad. They seek to empower people in every sphere of life to glorify God in body and spirit.

Dr. Rhonda Johnson with kindergarten MIPADEP children

In April 2016, the Triumph Church team painted the clinic, provided Bible instruction, conducted hygiene and health lessons at MIPADEP — along with medical and vision clinics, sewing lessons, and business classes to students at ETI. In 2017 and 2018, they continued their core educational, sewing, medical, vision, food, and clothing support activities.

HOPE THROUGH GOD'S WORD

Nothing in life brightens hope better than God's Word. We find therein inspiration for life's journey and sustenance to trust in God for all things. In God's Word, we happily discover God's plan for our lives.

According to the words of the prophet (Jeremiah 29:11, NLT), "'For I know the plans I have for you,' says the Lord. 'They are plans for good and not for disaster, to give you a future and a hope.'"

FLM Haiti's mission teams have always incorporated ministers who proclaim hope to God's people through prayer, preaching, and teaching. One of the greatest contributions of the Triumph Church team in shoring up hope was the addition of the pastors' seminar. It was led by Pastor Lee Haney, St. Paul Baptist Church, Donora, Pennsylvania; Pastor Craig Giles, Triumph Church, Pittsburgh; and Pastor Michael Stitt, Saints Memorial Baptist Church, Bryn Mawr, Pennsylvania; in collaboration with Bishop Leon Pamphile. It was a wonderful opportunity to equip the lamplighters of the community. (As many of our Haitian pastors did not have access to seminary training, they gladly welcomed the seminars as a way to sharpen their skills. These seminars were also an awesome manifestation of the ecumenical spirit, bringing together pastors of various denominations under one roof.)

In 2017, the seminar of Christian Leadership and Homiletics focused on the book of Nehemiah. This book holds answers that are important to today's ministry challenges. Nehemiah saw a problem, and he turned to God. God called him to rebuild the walls and gates of Jerusalem. Nehemiah left his job to do what God wanted him to do. It was not easy, but he kept going until the walls were rebuilt in just 52 days!

As leaders, pastors face many of the same challenges that Nehemiah did. They are confronted with challenges and are called to action. They are tested as leaders.

Rev. Lee Hainey and Leon at the pastor's seminar in Haiti

In this seminar, the pastors examined how Nehemiah's lessons applied to them. We all have our walls — things God puts on our hearts that we need to do as leaders. For Nehemiah, it literally was the building of a wall. The question posed in the seminar: "What is God asking us to do?"

The U.S. pastors shared that one modern-day "wall" they face are personal challenges to leadership. Just like the wall of Jericho — it is a challenge that needs to come down, as it hinders success and gets in the way of one's relationship with Christ. The seminar focused on how Nehemiah's lessons show that leadership can help solve any challenge.

The 2017 Triumph Mission Team Pastors' Seminar was attended by more than 40 Haitian pastors. Some traveled three hours in the wee hours of the morning to attend the sessions, which started at 8:30 a.m., ended at 11:30 a.m., and included a hearty breakfast and lunch. The Haitian pastors were surprised to receive a certificate and a stipend at the end of the week in appreciation for their participation. Each day, spirited devotions were led by

Haitian ministers. They prayed and discussed the daily lesson.

Mission team members at the clinic

Triumph mission team at the FLM guest house

Bishop Pamphile (rear), Pastor Giles (left), and Pastor Haney (right)

In 2018, more than 50 Haitian ministers attended the Pastors' Seminar of Christian Leadership and Homiletics, which centered on Paul's letter to the Ephesians. This is considered one of Paul's prison Epistles. He was a prisoner in Rome when he wrote the epistle to the Ephesians in about A.D. 60. He was writing to people he knew and loved, after he had spent more than two years teaching the Ephesian people (Acts 19:9-10). Since there are no personal greetings at the beginning of the letter, it is possible that this was intended to function as a circular letter for several churches in Asia Minor.

The book of Ephesians is written to Christians who don't understand the riches they have in Christ. As a Christian, are you aware of how rich you are? Do you know the full extent of the spiritual power offered to you to help you live a full Christian life? Paul's letter to the Ephesians has been an inspiration to new Christians as well as veterans in the faith. In this seminar, the pastors examined how the lessons of Ephesians applied to them.

Rev. Lee Hainey and paint team

PERSONAL REFLECTIONS
FROM THE PASTORS

During the weeks of the pastors' seminar, pastors Craig Giles, Lee Haney Sr., and Michael Stitt met for "Evening Reflections," a time of quietude, prayer, and worship. Some of the reflections of what the seminar teachers learned and observed are captured here:

- Endearing respect and honor for Bishop Pamphile by the Haitian pastors.

- How the Word of God and presence of the Holy Spirit created an atmosphere and spirit of unity.
- The bonding as "brothers and sisters in Christ."
- Enthusiasm and dedication to attending the seminar, demonstrated by the Haiti pastors.
- The pastors' appreciation for the meals provided daily.
- The worship experience daily transcended cultural and language barriers.
- Many pastors traveled long distances to attend, but were always on time and prepared. Many walked miles, and others had to take several 'tap-taps' to get there by 8 a.m.
- The experience of working with pastors who did not know how to read or write — yet had a vast knowledge of Scripture. These pastors knew the Bible just as well as many American pastors who have formal/advanced training.
- Enhanced awareness that the abundance of material possessions does not give peace and joy.
- A feeling that the pastors' seminar fostered and created a "blended family" experience.
- The atmosphere was not one of "teachers and students." There was mutual respect for one another and trust, all centered around our faith and belief in Jesus Christ.
- The inclusion of two women in the second year — which seemed to be somewhat "groundbreaking."

- In both years, there was never any dissension or conflict, and everything was executed flawlessly.

The pastors expressed their gratitude to have participated in the Triumph Church Haiti missions in 2016, 2017, and 2018. They enjoyed the broad scope of the missions and had multiple assignments, including participation in the educational missions in the schools, and working in the medical and vision clinics. Pastors Giles, Haney, and Stitt enjoyed all their work, from painting to providing spiritual guidance to the team members. Each Triumph team pastor had the privilege of preaching in a local church and experiencing what it was like to preach with translator assistance.

The Triumph teams have many special memories — getting through the airport with their many bags and supplies; conservation of their clean water supplies and a greater appreciation of electricity; appreciation for each member of the team and how their months of preparation made a very complicated mission work so well. Every team member knew their assignments, and they remained focused on their mission goals.

The pastors also enjoyed the cultural experiences of traveling through sections of Haiti, attending a soccer game, visiting the local art markets, and buying art from the vendors. The pastors appreciated the love and kindness extended to the Triumph team by the translation team, the transportation team, the churches they visited, the staff at the Kay D' Esperans Guest House — plus the staff at the various schools (MIPADEP, ETI) and the local community schools and clinics they visited.

NURTURING HOPE

Rev. Dr. Jim Moran and his wife, Dr. Lynn Moran, served on several missions trips in Haiti with

FLM. Their story is a manifest testimony of divine intervention in using them as instruments to promote hope not only in Haiti, but also with their constituents in the United States. This is the way Lynn described her initial connection with FLM:

"It was no accident that God sent me on my first trip to Haiti with my husband in January 2008. Upon returning to Pittsburgh, after spending 15 wonderful years in a ministry in Grove City, Ohio, I wanted to give something back to the pharmacy community in the city where I first began my career. One day, I called the University of Pittsburgh School of Pharmacy to inquire about a possible volunteer opportunity at a clinic. I was directed to the individual who managed the Free Clinics in Pittsburgh, and was told they could always use a pharmacist when open. I was matched with a clinic that met every other week under the direction of Dr. Bill Markle.

"His wife, Mary, worked there as a nurse as well, and welcomed me into the clinic. Toward the end of my first evening there, Mary came back to the pharmacy area with a packet of papers in hand. Her question to me, 'You would not happen to be interested in a medical mission to Haiti, would you? We really need a pharmacist on our team to set up our pharmacy in the new clinic opening there.' I told her I had never thought about it, but would certainly look over the materials.

"The next day, my husband came home from his church office. He said, unfortunately, that the educational trip we had planned to take the following January to the Holy Land had been canceled due to low numbers. It was the exact week of the medical mission trip I had just learned about from Mary, and the cost was within $10 of the Haiti trip cost. I shared the information with Jim that evening, and we decided it was no coincidence and that God was calling on us. That January, and many years after, we made that special trip to minister to the health and spiritual needs of our Haitian brothers and sisters as they ministered to us."

Now the Bible teaches that Peter and John, arrested for healing a lame man by the power of Jesus, testified with boldness: "For we cannot but speak the things which we have seen and heard" (Acts 4:20). Upon returning from Haiti, Rev. Moran was motivated to share what he had heard and seen with his congregation in Cranberry, Pennsylvania (a community not far from Pittsburgh). His wife, Lynn, relates how he wrestled with the challenge of making his experiences from each mission trip real to his congregation. She would say that, on the Sunday following his return from each of the mission trips, Pastor Jim would start the worship hour by sharing the highlights from his team's week in Haiti. When he spoke of his Haitian brothers and sisters in Christ, his eyes would naturally always sparkle, which made what he was saying so real to the listeners.

As the couple made more trips with the FLM Medical Mission, many in the church would send money with Pastor Jim to use for those he identified with a need during our time there. He would share with his congregation some of the personal stories of those who received their support. This included a child who was able to have a much-needed surgery, a mother or father who needed help to feed his or her family, an FLM interpreter who had a pressing family need, a guesthouse worker who needed a pair of shoes (since his had soles with huge holes), or the purchasing of extra pharmaceuticals FLM needed to use during the week — to mention only a few.

Lynn Moran added, "When Pastor Jim shared these stories, this helped his church to identify with the needs in Haiti in a personal way, and helped the congregation to always know how important their support was. When Pastor Jim communicated his report to his congregation, it was an experience that enhanced their faith — while, in turn, encouraging them to continue extending their support to their Haitian brothers and sisters. It was a manifestation of hope being mutually experienced both ways."

Birdy Reynolds' story about her calling to join FLM Haiti is a living testimony of God's guidance of the ministry. She writes:

"I woke up with a plan ... exercise and start dinner before going to church. I turned on my music and began to stretch. The first song to play was 'Launch Out' by Alvin Slaughter. The refrain of the song captured my attention ... 'Launch out into the deep, let your faith take you somewhere that you've never been before ...' I thought to myself, 'that's going to be my new motto in life.' I have always played it safe. Resistance to 'launching out' stems from my own insecurities and feelings of inadequacies, which have kept me safe on the shores of my life."

Birdy Reynolds

While exercising, Reynolds said that a part of her dream from the previous night flashed before her mind. "It was like a silent movie. I saw a Black man, with striking facial features, wearing a blue shirt with white flowers, sitting with his legs crossed cowboy style. He was leaning back, smiling. In front of him was a light brown, dirt area, and behind him looked like a blueprint for a construction site. It was a bright sunny day. The 'vision' stopped me momentarily, but I didn't think much more about it and continued exercising."

As she continued the day, Reynolds said the morning got away from her. She didn't make it to church, but watched the service on Livestream. It was missions Sunday. "Great," she thought. "If I had to miss a day, this was the day. Sad to say, I did not consider myself a missionary, and knew the service would be all about mission work.

Eva, the missions leader for our church, introduced Dr. Leon Pamphile, founder of the Functional Literacy Ministry in Haiti. I had never seen this person before, yet to my surprise, when I looked at the TV screen, I recognized him as the man in my dream! He was seeking educators for their summer missions trip, to provide quality professional development for the Haitian teachers."

Such a testimony of hope and obedience! Ever since that moment, over the past decade, Reynolds has been working to promote hope in Haiti, including a six-month stay in the country as FLM's first resident missionary.

HOPE THROUGH BUILDING RELATIONSHIPS

It has been said that relationships are better than money. FLM Haiti has been a ready conduit that helps build relationships between people across faith, ethnicity, and race. Mission team members bear witness of this precious reality. James Strang, whose contribution was highlighted, makes these reflections: "Over the past nine or so years, I have had the privilege to work with many truly outstanding people in the USA and Haiti. My life has been richly blessed through these associations. I rejoice in knowing that, together, we have been successful in accomplishing our mission to bring education, health care, and hope, through Christ, to many people in Haiti. Through many mission trips (as I worked side-by-side with the Haitian staff at the school, clinic, ETI, and guest house), I became more and more impressed with their eagerness to learn new skills — and to patiently teach me insights into a new culture.My old preconceived, stereotypical impressions crumbled. I developed some lasting friendships with truly beautiful people. As God's children, that which unites us is greater than that which separates us."

Dr. Robin McGuire, a Pittsburgh-area OB/GYN and a FLM board member, agrees that the mission trips provide "the opportunity to build relationships with our Haitian friends: to learn from them and help provide resources and training for Haitians, to provide education and health care in their communities."

Andy McCauley of Morgantown, West Virginia has made many mission trips to Haiti. He conveys that it was a blessing for team members to share their blessings there. He argued that God richly blesses mission team members in more ways than they realize when joining on a mission trip to Haiti: "You will gain a new appreciation for your current life. Through the grace and gratitude of the Haitian people, you will receive many more blessings than you can imagine."

As FLM volunteers and board members stand on a conviction of hope, they feel as if they are investing their time and resources in building the beloved community that the Lord Jesus had always envisioned.

Nicki Perfetti, a nurse who served on mission teams and on the board, commented, "The doctors, nurses, and other team members from all walks of life served the Haitians to the best of our ability, with all the resources we either brought or had available. It was amazing to see how a group of people who did not know each other came together to serve those less fortunate than ourselves and for the greater good."

Daniel Webster, the great American orator, once made a statement that conveys very well FLM's attitude, saying, "If we work upon marble, it will perish; if we work upon brass, time will efface it; if we rear temples, they will crumble into dust; but if we work upon immortal minds and instill into them just principles, we are then engraving that upon tablets which no time will efface, but will brighten and brighten to all eternity."

The board displayed — and continues to display — ongoing inspiration and courage to reach out and touch the less fortunate in Haiti. In the midst of despair, it is good to raise the banner of hope. As inspirational author, Horace Jackson Brown Jr., appropriately said, "Never deprive someone of hope; it may be all they have."

Hope has been at the core of this ministry. We believe that the horizon is always bright as we work together as a board. Through teamwork, we feel that God can unlock doors of opportunities for "the least of these our brothers" on the island of Haiti. We often refer to the story of Joseph, who was unjustly mistreated, spent time in jail, and was raised by God to a position where he worked for "the saving of many lives" (Genesis 50:20). FLM Haiti is fully engaged in the noble endeavor of saving lives.

CONCLUSION

FLM Haiti was launched in 1983 as a ministry designed to provide literacy skills to adults. It evolved through the years to offer so much more. It first began widening its scope by engaging in the education of youths through MIPADEP, a K-13 school of primary and secondary education. Soon, FLM ventured into the field of health care, and for more than a decade, the House of David has been a pillar in the community, responding to the healthcare needs of the population.

Shortly after the earthquake in January 2010, FLM networked with Building Goodness Foundation in providing houses for earthquake victims and homeless families. Through this partnership, the Excelsior Technical Institute was built as an academy to equip youth with skills for the reconstruction of the country — and with their own skills for entrepreneurship. A guesthouse was also built to accommodate missions teams. Kay D'Esperans (House of Hope) opened in 2011. Surrounded by fiery flamboyant trees, and adorned by bougainvillea blooms, the guesthouse provides safety and rest for human service workers coming to Haiti to help the Haitian people. It also serves as a community education center. In the wake of the cholera epidemics, FLM Haiti used the guesthouse to hold public seminars, to promote clean water as a means of controlling the disease.

In addition to the ongoing services rendered through its educational and healthcare facilities, FLM Haiti improves people's lives with the help of short-term mission teams. Twice a year, medical and educational teams from such cities as Buffalo, Miami, Boston, and Los Angeles travel to Haiti to provide medical care, teach Vacation Bible School and hold seminars for teachers. Over the past 20 years, more than 500 volunteers — using their own resources — have dedicated themselves to work in partnership with FLM to increase access to education and health care.

As a Christ-centered organization, FLM Haiti also strives to promote understanding between people of different faiths. Protestants, Catholics, and Jews have joined hands together to minister in Haiti. A team from the Rodef Shalom synagogue in Pittsburgh has served in Haiti. Dr. Ervin Dyer, of the University of Pittsburgh, and B. Denise Hawkins, a journalist based in Virginia, has led several communication teams across the Caribbean nation on tours dedicated to studying and showing Haitian culture in a more favorable light. FLM has been a channel in building healthy relationships between people across racial and religious barriers.

Kelly Eplee highlights the partnership between FLM and BGF. He argues, "I would like to credit FLM with providing the collaborative culture that pushed BGF to its own new heights, from adolescence to adulthood as it were. *Excelsior* indeed! As we review on the FLM website the many accomplishments and the ministry that FLM brings to Haiti, I cannot help but rejoice and be thankful for our time together. We gained great experience in these projects through mutual support, trust, and accountable communications. Hundreds of our volunteers will never be the same, and now live and build —knowing they have been a part of something great. We thank God and FLM and you, Bishop Leon Pamphile, for this opportunity to serve the people of Haiti and grow more fully into the people and builders we are created to be."

Ultimately, the preeminent goal of FLM Haiti is to help Haitians help themselves. FLM Haiti believes that the future of Haiti lies with its people. To that end, all of our efforts are designed to foster leadership and problem-solving with those we serve. We promote development of the skills necessary to seek or create employment, and to aid in making it possible for Haitians to raise their children to be healthy and productive citizens.

Dr. Ronald Peters, a Pittsburgh minister and educator, who's traveled with FLM to Haiti, helps to put our nonprofit's 40 years of service into perspective: "The Holy Bible's fourth Gospel closes with candid acknowledgment that there was much more than could be adequately written about Jesus' life on earth in the flesh (John 21:25). Yet, that Gospel, as with the other three, brims from beginning to end with testimonies of how Jesus' life fundamentally transformed human understanding of God's involvement in the world and throughout eternity. Similarly, the Holy Spirit's marvelous workings over the past 40 years, through the organization we know as the Functional Literacy Ministry, cannot be told adequately by mere documentation of activities, dates, statistics, challenges, and achievements. Neither can divine blessings, resulting from FLM, be fully disclosed only by documentation of the powerful, unparalleled, and visionary ministry of its illustrious founder, Bishop Leon Pamphile, the encouragement of his wife, Mrs. Rozelle Pamphile, the dedication of FLM staff, enthusiastic volunteers, and donors who joined in this mission across the years."

After 40 years of service in Haiti, it is evident that our task is far from finished. In *The Plague*, a literary classic of 20th-century world literature, Albert Camus related the siege of the city of Oran by a sudden epidemic of plague. At first, the citizens refused to accept the fact. But finally, the multiplication of deaths had to be acknowledged. The town was closed. Dr. Rieux, among others, committed himself to fighting the plague, which subsided after a season. But he was still resolute to be on his guard "in the never-ending fight against terror and its relentless onslaughts, knowing that the plague bacillus (bacteria) never dies or disappears for good."

Haiti remains a country deeply embedded in

poverty, and the fight against it is never-ending. To uproot poverty, Haiti needs to have strong institutions, transparent governments, a strong educational system, political stability, equitable distribution of resources, and so forth. The country is far from meeting these prerequisites to mount a strong campaign against poverty. In the present context, Haiti is in the throes of a serious humanitarian crisis. According to the World Food Program (WFP), "nearly half of the Haitian population, or 4.9 million people, are struggling to feed themselves." This figure has tripled compared to 2016. Galloping inflation makes it impossible to buy basic food products for millions of Haitians, while, according to the World Bank, Haiti is one of the 10 countries most affected by food price inflation.

Solutions to Haiti's socioeconomic problems require a paradigm shift in the overall attitude of the political and economic elite of the country toward its citizens. They need to focus on respecting the right of every Haitian to basic human dignity, and their right to basic services in health, education, and welfare. Jesus addressed this issue saying, "You know that the rulers of the Gentiles lord it over them, and their high officials exercise authority over them. Not so with you. Instead, whoever wants to become great among you must be your servant" (Matthew 20:25-26, NIV). The spirit of love and servanthood must be the foundation of the rebuilding of a better Haiti.

I find great inspiration in the words of Solomon: "The generous will prosper; those who refresh others will themselves be refreshed" (Proverbs 11:25, NLT). I am greatly refreshed by the privilege of founding and leading the Functional Literacy Ministry of Haiti for the past 40 years. Testimonies abound that those who have joined this effort have also been blessed and refreshed. We are compelled by love to see the fulfillment of the vision of dignity, self-worth, and self-respect for every Haitian and every human being.

ACKNOWLEDGMENTS

Ever since its creation in 1983, the Functional Literacy Ministry of Haiti has evolved as a true example of teamwork. It is a living testimony that when people work together, they can achieve the extraordinary. Though this book is primarily written using FLM board minutes, reports, and newsletters, it is also the fruit of cooperation of FLM's former and current board members, and especially mission team members who made things happen on the ground.

First, I want to thank God for the longstanding support of my wife and FLM advocate, Rozelle Pamphile. Her continued commitment has made much of what we do possible.

Second, I want to express my gratitude to others for their contribution to the writing of the FLM story. I am particularly indebted to Dr. Ervin Dyer, who, as the co-author of this book, has provided guidance and served as the editor. Russell Bynum, the Deputy Executive Director, has handled the graphic design and layout. Let me further acknowledge the following people, who also shared their experiences as board and mission team members in Haiti:

Russell Bynum	Nicki Perfetti
Susan Robinson	Kelly Eplee of the
Birdy Reynolds	Building Goodness
Dr. Lynn Moran	Foundation (BGF)
Dr. Rhonda Taliaferro	Dr. Bill Markle
Dr. Robin McGuire	Dr. Rhonda Johnson
Jim Strang	Dr. Ronald Peters
Howard Rich of Churches	Marian Allen
in Action (CIA)	Isabel Smith

May these volunteers, and others who have made possible the writing of the FLM story, find here the expression of my deepest gratitude.

Excelsior,
Bishop Leon D. Pamphile, Ph.D
Founder/Executive Director, FLM Haiti

METHODOLOGY

History, statistics, and other information were drawn from newspapers, history sources, and Dr. Pamphile's own independent research.

Cover Caption: A Haitian woman makes her way to one of FLM Haiti's medical missions in 2018. Photo by Kenneth Neely.

About Kenneth Neely:
Kenneth Neely is a visual storyteller who uses photography and mixed media paintings to tell the rich, and often complex, stories of people of color. He is fueled by love, passion, God-given talent, and more than 30 years of experience.

His work has been included in several exhibits, including "Picturing the City: Downtown Pittsburgh" with the Heinz Endowments at The Carnegie Museum of Art, and "Welcome to Pittsburgh" at Boom Concepts Gallery in Garfield. His additional gift is teaching art and uncovering the artistic talent that children inherently have. He has worked with children for more than 10 years and has served as the resident artist at The Mount Ararat Community Activity Center, where he taught art to children between the ages of 3 to 14.
Currently, he serves as an art instructor at Imani Christian Academy.

See more at: www.kneelyimages.com

Cover and Interior Book Design:
Bynums Marketing & Communications, Inc.

Works by
Dr. Leon D. Pamphile

WorldCat credits Dr. Leon D. Pamphile with 15 works in 57 publications, in two languages and 3,102 library holdings. These include:

HISTORICAL WORKS

- Haitians and African Americans: A Heritage of Tragedy and Hope
- Contrary Destinies: A Century of America's Occupation, Deoccupation and Reoccupation Of Haiti
- Clash of Cultures: America's Educational Strategies in Occupied Haiti, 1915-1934
- La Croix et Le Glaive: l'Eglise Catholique et l'occupation Américaine d'Haiti, 1915-1934
- L'Education en Haiti sous L'Occupation Américaine, 1915-1934
- Les Racines des Relations Haïtiano-Américaines
- Deux Destins Contraires: un Siècle D'Occupation, de Desoccupation et de Reoccupation Américaine d'Haiti

INSPIRATIONAL AND MOTIVATIONAL WORKS

- The Mind of Christ: Your Weapon of Victory
- Adjusting to Life's Changing Seasons
- Well-Being Through Well-Doing
- 101 Keys for Victorious Living

For more information on
FLM Haiti
or to donate, go to:
www.FLMHaiti.org/donate

Made in the USA
Monee, IL
14 October 2023

44287447R10090